FRIDAY

DISCOURSES

Jum'ah Talks at the Rasooli Center

Volume 1

SHAYKH FADHLALLA HAERI

Zahra Publications

ISBN-13 (Printed Version): 978-1-92-832936-7

First Published in 2012

Second Edition Published by Zahra Publications
Distributed and Published by Zahra Publications
PO Box 50764
Wierda Park 0149 Centurion
South Africa
www.zahrapublications.pub

Designed and typeset in South Africa by Quintessence Publishing
Cover Design by Quintessence Publishing
Project Management by Quintessence Publishing

Set in 11 point on 16 point, Adobe Garamond Pro

TABLE OF CONTENTS

BOOK DESCRIPTION

These talks were delivered over a series of Friday prayer gatherings at the Rasooli Center, Centurion, south of Pretoria, South Africa. Shaykh Fadhlalla Haeri boldly addresses many topics that influence Muslims at the core of what it means to be a Muslim in today's global village and how to be transformed by living the *Din* of Islam truly. With his finger on the pulse of our times, Shaykh Fadhlalla Haeri highlights the critical issues with a sense of urgency, clarity of insight and guidance grounded in the Qur'an and Prophetic way. These challenges ultimately revolve around the core science of self-knowledge and awakening to the inner potential within us to live in harmony with God's decree of unity, justice and mercy.

ABOUT THE AUTHOR

Shaykh Fadhlalla Haeri was born in Karbala, Iraq, a descendant of several generations of well-known and revered spiritual leaders. Educated in Europe and America, he founded a number of companies in the Middle East and worked as a consultant in the oil industry.

He travelled extensively on a spiritual quest which led to his eventual re-discovery of the pure and original Islamic heritage of his birth.

In 1980 he established the Zahra Trust, a charitable organization with centers in the USA, Britain and the Middle East, which makes traditional Islamic teachings more widely available through courses and publications, promotes the revival of traditional systems of healing and supports a variety of charitable programs.

Shaykh Fadhlalla is currently engaged in lecturing and writing books and commentaries on the Holy Qur'an and related subjects, with particular emphasis on ethics, self-development and gnosis (`irfan).

In 2004, he established the Academy of Self Knowledge, http://www.askonline.co.za, which offers teachings on self knowledge and the Prophetic revealed path.

ACKNOWLEDGMENTS

The Rasooli Center was built and developed as a collective effort by several intimate friends and seekers of truth and enlightenment. The early core of supporters were Ibrahim Ravat, Haroun Ebrahim, Farhad Joosub, Younus Ismail and their families. Soon the number of serious and generous people grew to include Abu Bakr Karolia, Omar Essa, several members of the Kalla family and a few dozens more. The Jum'ah talks became a venue for serious teachings of the *Qur'ān* and the *Din*. For these talks, their recording and transcription, special thanks are due to Younus Ismail, Sajidah, Dr. Zaheer Adham, Zaheer Cassim, Nusra Cassiem and Muna Bilgrami.

INTRODUCTION

Islam is based on the belief that there is One Compassionate, All-encompassing God; that the purpose of creation is to recognize, desire and embrace his great qualities and attributes, all of which emanate from His essence which is the power behind the universe. Thus our primary and urgent business is the knowledge of Allah, His ways, designs and attributes, and the experience of transformation that follows through reflection and insights. All other human pursuits are secondary.

The spread of early Islam purified old cultures from past unjust or unnatural habits and conditioning. Many of the acceptable customs and traditions were improved by Islam and were allowed to continue. In time a dynamic Islamic culture emerged with regional variations and flavors.

Islam connects the material and discernible world with that which is unseen and considered sacred. The human being is the meeting point between a physical micro-cosmos and the universal macrocosm and Allah's eternal light. The culture of any people is based upon sets of values and perceptions, which motivate them to behave in a particular way over a long period of time. There are several factors that underlie the distinctiveness of the Muslim culture but the most predominant of all is the belief in the eternal Oneness which connects and governs the universe.

It is primarily the *dīn* and courtesy of Islam – the behavioral patterns, practices, and perceptions of life – that have influenced the Muslim peoples and brought about the basic foundations of an 'Islamic way of life', with variation in culture and social habits. Islam's bedrock is the belief in the One All-embracing God and that this life is a preparation for the hereafter, which is shaped by the quality of life and conduct on earth.

When different races, tribes, and nations assimilate the *dīn* deeply and correctly, one finds that they first identify themselves as Muslims before nations, societies, or races. Equally, when Islam is not deeply rooted in a people, the national, racial, cultural, or other group identities take precedence over their faith to the detriment of its application.

The modern world presents new ways and greater complexities, chaos, constant change and challenges our values and way of life. Therefore, what is needed is the rediscovery of Allah's patterns as revealed in the *Qur'ānic* message and translated into action through the prophetic way. The life of a conscientious seeker is far more refined and attuned to the heart, where the soul resides which brings about awareness, accountability, insights and fulfilled beingness.

The following discourses were given during a period of some ten years at the Rasooli Mosque in Raslouw and were transcribed and edited by several friends and students. Please note that it is customary to invoke the peace and blessings of Allah upon the Prophet every time his name is mentioned. While we have not included such mentions for reasons of print economy since we mention him so often, we hope the reader will nonetheless ask Allah for such blessings, and thereby bask in the reflection of the prophetic light. While most Arabic words used have been explained within the text, a glossary has also been included. Translations from the *Qur'ān* have been modified from a selection including those by Yusuf Ali and Shakir.

These Friday talks were given from heart to heart and I hope they will inspire the reader to think and act with greater awareness, better intention and action.

I: THE GLORY OF ISLAM

Islam provides us with the appropriate maps and prescriptions to relate to the outer world successfully whilst enabling the heart to be wholesome and joyful.

All of us know that as Muslims we submit to Allah – to His Light, His Power, His Knowledge – because we are not independent, but dependent on Him. The child is dependent on its mother and upon reaching maturity transfers this dependency to the Higher. Self-aware parents will admit to their limitations by recognizing that they were acting as *Rabb* (Lord), in the place of the Lord, and therefore as *khalīfah* (representative of Allah), but a time has come that the children's potential outstrips that of the parents. Their prayer becomes, therefore, that somehow the children will become better than them, that there is only One *Rabb* and we are merely trying to act by proxy, as guardians.

This aspect of submission, or our dependency on the Creator, is one of a half dozen foundations of the *dīn*. If we do not understand them, we will not be able to build anything of our *dīn* upon them. Another major foundation is that we are always trying to attract to ourselves what we like and avoid that which we do not like – this is to do with obedience and living in harmony with attaining the higher goals of what it means to be human. What we may like now may be to do with our lower self – our ego, our stomach or something else – but ultimately if we want to bring ourselves to light or higher knowledge then what we like should be a good objective. Avoiding evil, doubt, misery, or ill health is a part of that. We must encourage that which we like and avoid that which we do not like, provided it is not 'we' anymore, but the higher in us that decides what is appropriate for us and what is not.

These are basic foundations from the *Qur'ān* and the way of the Prophet. If you can understand them then I can share with you the foundations of the glory of our *dīn*, not the glory of Muslims. On occasion Muslims have acted gloriously and at other times perversely. Soon after the departure of the Prophet, a lot of unnecessary tension and new ignorance came to the fore, for which, in a way, we are all still paying the price now. We have inherited the entire legacy of the light of Muhammad together with the ignorance of many communities and their inadvertent mistakes.

We cannot avoid facing our past. As human beings, we are the recipients of the entire consciousness of humanity, from the rise of our father, Adam, to all the other thousands of prophets until now. We cannot deny the effect of this upon us. As Muslims we want to be proud of our heritage and yet we find so much of our previous generations' conduct and, indeed, even some of the conduct that goes on presently in the Middle East and elsewhere unacceptable. At a human level it is unacceptable, let alone at the spiritual level. As a result, many of us are confused. Many of us act as if we know Islam is the greatest, but then we are also disappointed or upset by the conduct of the Muslims and our own conduct because we are the same.

The glory of Islam can only be regained if we adhere to Allah's ways. Allah's ways are based on *la ilāha illa'llāh* – denying falsehood and acknowledging truth: no god BUT Allah. We cannot do one without the other. We cannot have any experience in life unless it is based on 'no' to that which is not right and 'yes' to that which is right. Then we are in balance. The glory of Islam will only be regained and become effulgent if each one of us as Muslims, as individuals, as families and as communities, realize what is to be avoided and what is to be encouraged.

What we are suffering most from nowadays, as was the case in the past, is ignorance or 'darkness'. This is the situation of human beings:

☼ 'I swear by Time: Most surely man is in loss.'
[103:1-2]

The first thing we should say no to is ignorance and to being stubbornly attached to what we are used to in the past simply because of what our fathers or somebody else said or did. The banner of Islam was raised amongst people who were the most ignorant – the Arabs of those days – at a time when there was maximum darkness by a being who was in every way illuminated and taken into the divine precinct. We therefore have to be vigilant of ignorance. If the ignorance involves only one person, the effect is not too bad, but when it involves a whole community or becomes an attribute of certain teachers, leaders, rulers or religious scholars (*'ulama*), then it can be catastrophic, because its effect is far more dominating and dangerous.

This has been the case for centuries with many of us. Be aware of it. Simply because a person has a platform or a big name or a big turban, it does not mean that he is in every way truly a seeker (*sālik*) on the path, or that he is truly under the protection of Allah's *rahmah* and is yielding to his *īmān* (faith and belief in Allah), acting in *ihsān* (perfect conduct) and ready to leave this world. We have to evaluate it and judge it for ourselves.

If we are to regain any of the glories of the way of our Prophet the first step is the removal of all falsehood. This was the case in Makkah. The removal of falsehood took place in Makkah when the Prophet came. Most of the *āyāt* (*Qur'ānic* verses) revealed in Makkah were about action: verses exhorting people to wake up, reflect, ponder, look at the sky and the heavens and other signs, and acknowledge death. We are told to listen to this voice of *Haqq* (Truth), for it is to do with *haqiqah* (truth and reality). The Prophet addressed everyone in Makkah, as if spreading pearls before the oceans of humanity.

To remove falsehood in Muslim communities now, first and foremost, we must remove our fantasies or assumptions or presumption about worship. This is the cause of all the unnecessary hair-splitting disputes between the different *madhahib* (schools of Islamic jurisprudence, pl. of *madhhab*). If you perfect your worship, then you realize that Allah is in charge of you and Allah is in charge of other people. Then you wonder why they are causing so much damage. Allah enables us to choose and allows us to cause damage so that eventually we have to stop. The earth is Allah's kindergarten: Allah's ways and laws are like a master of a kindergarten who allows the inmates to make mistakes up to a certain point, beyond which as Allah says:

☼ '...Allah will bring a people whom He loves and who love Him...' [5:54]

Human history takes place in cycles. The Mongols set out to destroy the Muslims. For nearly eighty years they had the upper hand over Muslims. They nearly finished them off, but twenty or thirty years after that the Mongols themselves embraced Islam and enhanced the glory of Islam even more than before. Look at the cycles that go on in our lives. It is Allah's way. It is nature that will dictate what will prevail. You cannot go against Allah's nature. Animals have to learn how to conduct themselves and they often do from their genetic imprint. We human beings need to learn it much more than other animals: in the first seven years we have to learn to play; in the next seven years we have to learn what is allowed and what is not, what is correct and what is wrong; and in the third seven years we have to apply it. By the time we are twenty one we should know what to do and what not to do and our parents may continue to accompany us to make sure that we are following the ways of nature. That is our *dīn*. The first step towards perfecting worship is to remove falsehood from it. Allah loves those who are humble, who trust in Allah and who surrender to Allah. Worship is not about the number of times you have stood up to pray, nor how many prostrations you have made, nor how many times you have read the *Qur'ān* or recited it aloud. It is about the quality of your trusting, yielding, loving and giving in. Even if you do not know about the *dīn*, Allah will send you those who will come and show you. Love, trust, submission, knowledge that Allah is here, Allah was here, Allah will be here and that you are created to appreciate Him, know Him, love Him, adore Him, give in to Him, dive into Him and live by Him – that is worship.

The second step is to correct our relationships. Again, we Muslims assume that relationships are set in a certain way and that women have to be told what to do and their only role is to be locked behind the kitchen sink or in the nursery. A similar situation exists in relationships with our parents, our friends and at work. We are least clear about how our relationships at work should be. We do not understand that the people who are working with us are like our younger brothers, sons or daughters.

So to understand how far we have gone wrong we have to re-examine the relationships of the great ones – how the Prophet treated his people, how the great *Sahābas* (Companions of the Prophet) treated them, how the great Imams (Righteous Leaders) and the *Awliyā'* (Saints) treated their people. We are all equal in the eye of Allah, but not equal in our abilities or skills or other worldly or esoteric knowledge. We have to accept that, but as far as Allah is concerned we are all the same. We have come here in order to leave. These are the fundamental parameters of proper *mu'āmalāt* (transactions).

The third most important thing we have to remove in terms of falsehood is the poor quality of leadership. Who are those who are qualified to lead us? If a person himself is not healthy, how can he give you some advice about your health? If a person himself is completely confused in his mind, how can he help you sort out your confusion? Leadership implies those who are able to lead themselves. How? By recognizing who is the real leader of it all, who is the Creator of it all and what are His ways, His intentions and His purpose. In other words, the best and the most qualified leaders are those who have recognized the predominance, dominance, omnipotence, and omnipresence of Allah and then they can take counsel in terms of worldly matters. Our glorious Prophet always took counsel on worldly matters, but then he took the decision.

These are the ways that we can remove our falsehood. You may claim, 'I am a Muslim. I know the *Qur'ān*. I have even contributed to some mosque.' But are you free from fear of creation and of provision? Are you fearful of the Creator of it all? Are you in *taqwa* (cautious awareness arising from the love of Allah)? If you are, then you are fine. Otherwise, you will move endlessly from pillar to post, from one mosque to another, from one teacher to another.

The next part of this program of truly glorifying our *dīn* (the transaction of our life) is to live our *dīn* by establishing the truth. As you remove falsehood, you are establishing the truth – they go hand in hand. *La ilāha illa'llah* – there is no god BUT God. In Madinah the *dīn* was fully practiced. People were told, 'You cannot do this. You must not do that. You must watch out. Other people are like you so treat them as you would wish to be treated.' From Makkah we have moved from that which was open to everyone, which is the whole of Makkah, to the courtesy of Madinah, to establishing the truth in its fullness.

The truth is found at various levels: at the physical, the mental, the heart and the spiritual level – in fact at all levels. There is a truth in all of them, which is that there is one truth that never ever change, and that is the absolute foundation of the *Nūr* (Light) of Allah. Everything has truth in it: you have a toothache, it is real. There is a toothache, yes, but hopefully it will not last, so its truth is delineated by time. The removal of falsehood brings us alongside the establishment of the truth. The two go together.

The first foundation for knowledge of truth for Muslims is the knowledge of *Qur'ān* and the *Qur'ānic* fundamentals. The *Qur'ānic* fundamentals are essential. Most of our young people do not have a clue about the *dīn* because we have not given them the foundations of the *Qur'ān*. In order to approach the *Qur'ān* we have to be pure. Pure in what way? Pure in having neither presumption nor assumption. If we approach the *Qur'ān* as if we were ready to die then we will be amazed every time we read it. Every time we come to it we will find it fresh. If we come to it with a presumption or assumption, we will only see it through the veil of that presumption and assumption and, therefore, misconception. If we come to it free of any energy or possibility that we attribute to ourselves, we should ask Allah's guidance and read it in an attitude that says: 'O Allah, I am the most wretched and you are the most Glorious. Cover my wretchedness by Your Glory.' We will then see wonder upon wonder.

The second foundation, which goes hand in hand with it the *Qur'ānic*, is the way of the Prophet and that is not only the *Sunnah* (the prophetic practice) but also the *Sīrah* (the life of the Prophet), that is, the way he acted based not only on his authority and the verbal and linguistic injunctions of *Hadith* (Prophetic traditions), but also how he acted, what he said, how he said it, to whom he said it, and whether it was only on that special occasion that he said it or whether it referred to all times. The way of the Prophet which comes to us with the love of the Prophet, abandonment to the Prophet, submission to the Prophet and silence in the presence of the Prophet.

The third most important foundation is self-knowledge, particularly for our young people. Who are we? Why do we constantly look for this, that and the other? How reliable are we? One moment we are in a good mood and the next in a bad one, so which is the good part of us? Each one of us will reach a conclusion that there is within us a platform or a dimension that never ever changes and that is called *rūh* (the soul). We are a *rūh* caught in the prison of the body which has a *nafs* (self/ego). And the *nafs* is *ammāratum bi's-sū'* – it always takes us hither, thither and nowhere, confusing us. But then we also have a *Qalb* (heart) and within the *Qalb* there is a *Shāhid* (a witnesser), there is a *Raqīb* (the monitoring self) and there is a *Qarīn* (the recording companion). All these terms and the functions they stand for come from the *Qur'ān*.

We must understand the cosmology that is within us so that we can transcend it. When we learn to recognize these different elements at play we can negotiate with ourselves – *'I know you bring me down all the time. I know you want to pounce on others and take a pound of flesh off them, but look back at the last twenty years: how many times have you done that and what did you get out of it? Nothing but misery. So stop it!'*

Knowledge of the self revives the *dīn*. If we know ourselves – the lower self and the higher self – and transcend it, that is called 'living Islam'. We live it without talking about it anymore. There are no longer 'Islamic schools'. You do not lock Islam up in a museum or in a *madrasah*. It is alive! It is natural to make mistakes. But even though we may make them, if we are able to remain on that carpet of the humility born of our recognition and remorse, then we are in our *mihrab* (prayer niche), which is the place for war against the self (the *nafs*). *Mihrab* comes from the verb *haraba*, to wage war against ignorance, arrogance and assumption, and to wage war against the lower tendencies in us. When we engage with ourselves in that way then with our full-fledged, dynamic inter-active potential we are waking up to the *nūr* (light) of Allah. The light of Allah is potentially in every heart. When we alive to it, then we will be living Muslims.

If we are living Muslims, then for us *Īmān* (faith and trust) is a foundation and for us *Ihsān* (perfect conduct) is none other than the doctrine and Highway Code by which we are living because that at any second we are aware we may leave this world. Then the question remains: Are we leaving it contentedly or do we still have accounts to be rendered?

The glory of Islam is with us, but we Muslims must rise to it. Islam has always been glorious. Islam is nothing other than the essence of victory in this life and total eternal joy in the next life, provided we are up to it. This is something we cannot inherit. We have to take it by determination, perseverance, and abandonment. It has to be the sole *qiblah*.

'Allah does not change the condition of a people until they change what is within themselves.' [13:11]

2: THE REVIVAL OF
THE MUSLIMS

Muslims are the people who consider themselves adherent to the path of Islam. Some of them are Muslim by name, others are transformed by faith, worship and conduct.

We are living at a time where changes in the world are taking place rapidly in every way – economic, cultural and otherwise. Like being adrift in the middle of an ocean, the winds and waves are coming from every direction. We have been impacted on a personal level, on a family level and across societies and communities. No matter who you are or where you are, you cannot but feel the winds that are buffeting you. Wherever Muslims are – from China to the Atlantic, in Europe or in Africa – we are all feeling the same chilling winds.

Human beings are weak. The *Qur'ān* tells us on numerous occasions that we have been created weak and at a loss, without inner strengths, permanent rooting or resolve. Therefore, as weak human beings, we have a tendency to want to find a 'quick fix'. Like an elderly sick patient who is prescribed aspirin in the hopes of him starting to walk again and live normally and healthily, with full vitality within a few short minutes – it cannot be.

We must take the pulse of the patient and look into his history. We must then come up with a plan to change the *dis*-ease to ease, illness to wellness. It will not come overnight. The patience we need is like that of a mother. She carries a child for nine months in the womb, and then for the rest of her life – once a mother, forever a mother. In the first few years she has almost total responsibility which never ceases. The father also takes pride in his child and says: 'I am the father,' as though he has done a lot. Yet this poor woman endured sleepless nights and countless anxieties and along comes the father claiming proudly: 'Now look at my son!'

We must look deeply into the situation of the world. How did it come to be where it is now? In the West it is very easy for us to discern the major changes from the so-called Reformation and the development of the work ethic, to the separation of the moral or religious values of the church from the secularized state system. By 1694 in Britain, because of the Cromwellian era, this process was completed by the establishment of the Central Bank. It was privately owned, but the Government was the agent of ensuring that money was collected for repayment of its debt. The full establishment of the world hegemony of the money-makers and the banks was thus firmly set in motion. Subsequent developments were the natural results of this. With the advent of the French Revolution and the subsequent Bolshevik Revolution, the banks finally became fully and totally in control of people's lives. The politicians were simply there to ensure the stability of the economic system. So they were eventually in a position of mainly implementing policies that would enhance the continuity of the system, not reforming or changing it. By the Second World War most of the world was completely and utterly in the hands of the financial institutions and banks, and therefore the corporate institutions; politicians became scorekeepers and maintainers of the status quo. So the natural split of moral values from secular systems resulted in a very clear dichotomy in the West.

Until about 1750, we in the East or in the Muslim world still had, on the face of it, almost equal civilization, power and abilities. Within 50 years, by 1800, the balance was completely and irrevocably overturned. This is in reference to the social scene. But equal and parallel to the social, world or community scene, is the personal scene. From then onward we in the East also became totally subject to the control of the banking hegemony. Between 1860 and 1890 the bankers loaned enough money to the Egyptians, the Ottomans, and the governments in Iran, Morocco and Tunis and, to a lesser extent, other countries, to result in their gaining control over their governments' functions. Thus, if a Government was about to default, foreign powers had a very good reason for military intervention and to take over, a fact which the rulers of the affected regions knew very well. Thus the rulers in the Muslim world ended up as puppets in the hands of the global banking system.

We call ourselves Muslims but what does that mean? We have so much about this in our traditions from the prophetic teachings, from the *Qur'ān* and from the conduct of the blessed Prophet, his companions (*Sahābah*), his household (*Ahl ul-Bayt*), and others. We know a Muslim is he who has truly and utterly confessed *haqq* (truth) and admits the truth that we are indeed weak; that he has nothing of his own and that other people are safe from his tongue or his hand, so much so that he is cautious all his life; he is in cautious awareness and abstention (*taqwa*), and knows that he is a guest in this world. He has come by his Lord and is returning to his Lord. So the Muslim ends up being a true *mu'min* (believer): at peace within himself and at peace with other people.

The true *mu'min* will eventually become a *muhsin*. A *muhsin* is one who knows that though he may not 'see' Allah, Allah sees everything, Allah records everything and Allah knows everything. The *muhsin* has no secret agendas. He is clear. He possesses a *qalbun salīm* (a clear heart). The light in his heart will guide him because Allah tells us in the *Qur'ān* that the path to understanding, the path to knowing, the path to being with Allah, the path to being illumined by Allah is one of submission. Submit to the truth that we have come here to die.

Submitting to the truth means that the more we know, the more we come to know that we don't know. This is the condition of the

Muslim. He or she is alive, not pompous, not like these structured personalities who boast, 'Don't you know who I am?' At the end of the day, the ultimate question is 'Who are you really?' All we can say is: 'I am not really this. I play a role as a father, but I am not just a father. I am a teacher, but I am not just a teacher. I am a person who enjoys doing his *salāt*, but I am not only doing that. I am passing on part of Allah's *rahmah* (mercy) that has come to me.' And Allah says: *'The way to Allah is submission,'* meaning all of the religions are Islam. They have come at different times, through different cultures, languages and different prophets or messengers. There were thousands of them. Nothing has changed in this existence.

The only advantage we have is that the last of all of the prophets and messengers, Muhammad, introduced a package that we can apply at anytime, anywhere. That is the meaning of *khātama'l-anbiyā'i wa'l-mursalīn* [33:40] – the seal of the Prophets and the messengers, i.e. his message encompasses everything that went before. That is the advantage we have. Therefore, we also have the responsibility of that advantage of being enlightened.

Irrespective of the environment we are in, we must remember the early years in Makkah. A few Muslims were surrounded by enemies. Everybody around them was against them. How did they survive? We are living in a situation similar to the first few years of the Makkan community with added complications, but also with the advantage of knowing about Madinah and the glorious rise of Islam in different communities, cities and environments and what Islamic leadership was and should be. Whenever we look at the history of the Muslims and the leaders were prophetic, we find that the community grew both in this world and in preparation for the next world. Whenever that balance was disturbed, they became *Ahl al-dunya* (people attached to this material world) and too concerned about organizing this world and money, commerce, buildings and states. When this happens, we find that the community falters and weakens and gets recycled.

Thus the history of the Muslims is basically about the *dīn*. The Muslim is he who takes on the *dīn*, which means path or way. The *Qur'ān* is the atlas of life and therefore it is the foundation of this *dīn*. It is like going into a city we don't know: we want to get to the palace of the King, but if we don't have a map we will go this way and that and may go down a cul-de-sac which we cannot back out of, and sometimes we get stuck. The Prophet says: *'Do not enter through a doorway unless you know how to come out of it.'* So a Muslim is he who has absorbed the *Qur'ān*. He will then truly become a companion of the Prophet. He will become an *Ahl al-Bayt* (member of his household). When the Prophet put his arm around Salman-al-Farsi, he said: *'He is from us, the family of the Prophet.'* Family is not just a blood relationship. In our community we have amongst us some wonderful relationships with people whom we did not know even two years ago. It is our new family, our family by choice. With our blood family, we have no choice. Some cousins and uncles might be the worst of creation, as it was with the Prophet. We can generate a vibrant new family by our choosing people who are committed to the path of Islam, submission, enlightenment and being illumined by that certainty in our lives that Allah is our guide. Allah will always guide us.

Differences come by transgression, affliction and argument. Allah then says, talking again about the illumined Muslim: *'Is he who was dead then We raised him to life and made for him a light by which he walks among the people, like him whose likeness is that of one in utter darkness whence he cannot come forth? Thus what they did was made fair seeming to the unbelievers'* [6:122]. The first part of this verse implies that we are biologically dead – *'Is he who was dead then We raised him to life....'* If we are only concerned about our existential bodies and our minds and are not illumined, if we have not discovered that we are a *rūh*, we <u>are</u> dead. The question posed differentiates between whoever is brought to life again by his inner awakening and illuminated consciousness and one like *'him whose likeness is that of one in utter darkness whence he cannot come forth?'* Being in darkness implies denial of the truth and the purpose of existence. Furthermore, for those who deny this truth of purpose, *'what they did was made fair seeming'* to themselves. Humans are wired in such a way that we cannot live if we are not content with what we are doing, irrespective of whether it is the path of *haqq* or the path of falsehood. Self-justification is easy to slip into. Once we know that the atlas is the *Qur'ān* and that the map is being read and followed by the great Muslims, primarily by the prophets, then we want to follow the map to arrive in the presence of the King of kings, which is *hudūr* (Allah's presence and Allah's light). Allah indicates that once you live in that light and by that light, *'wherever you turn, there is Allah: surely Allah is Ample-giving, Knowing.'* [2:115]

Whatever situation we are in, Allah has made it possible for us to be in it, so that we beg Allah to get out of it. We recognize that Allah is the Doer; so our *tawhīd* becomes perfected and we only see One. Our condition is that we experience two states. Gradually we recognize the One behind the two. The Muslim is awakened by his *īmān*, constantly exerting *jihād*. The word *jihād* is from the Arabic verb whose noun is *jahd*, or expending energy and effort. Allah says: *'...they shall strive hard in Allah's way and shall not fear the censure of any censurer; this is Allah's grace, He gives it to whom He pleases, and Allah is Ample-giving, Knowing.'* [5:54]

The Muslim uses the *Qur'ān* as his atlas. He applies his *dīn* in full, in faith and in worship, confirming and accepting the *hudūd* (limits & boundaries) and *shari'ah* (revealed code of conduct), constantly acting correctly and asking himself: 'Am I doing the right thing? Is it the right time? Is it the right place?' By doing so he or she increases their energy and yearning for Allah, refining their focus so that Allah is called upon in *du'ā* (supplication): *'Rabbanā lā tuzigh qūlūbanā ba'da idh hadaytanā'* (*Our Lord! make not our hearts to deviate after You have guided us aright, and grant us from You mercy; surely You are the most liberal Giver*) [3:8]. Are we giving Allah an order by saying *'lā tuzigh qūlūbanā'* (Do not cause our hearts to deviate)? We are simply asking Allah to keep our hearts illumined. Therefore we beseech Him to not let our hearts fall under the tyranny of the *nafs* so that we can maintain our spiritual growth.

Then Allah says: *'Lan tanālu'l-birra hattā tanfaqū mimmā tūhibbūn'* (*By no means shall you attain to righteousness until you spend [benevolently] out of what you love; and whatever thing you spend, Allah surely knows it*) [3:92]. *Birr* is sincerity, honesty, loyalty and the root is related to barr which is open space, infinite desert. The implicit connection in meaning is that if you truly give of what you love, you will experience inner expansion. We are loyal to the conviction that we had nothing, we have come from nowhere, and we are returning to Him by whose grace and mercy we have come. So unless you expend of what you <u>love</u>, you cannot attain to that blessed state. This is the failing of the *kufr* system and the West because they do not give that which they want. They want the *dunyā* and Allah gives them the *dunyā*, though: *'... they shall have no portion in the Hereafter'*.

☼   So when you have performed your devotions, then remember Allah as you remembered your fathers, rather a profounder remembrance. But there are some people who say, Our Lord! Give us in the world, and they shall have no portion in the Hereafter. [2:200]

But what about us Muslims? Why is it we have not developed a system that is truly an alternative to the *kufr* system? Where is it that we have gone wrong? These are the questions we need to ask, but giving quick, glib answers in the hope that we can solve all our problems with a few useless, suicide attacks is not going to work. We have to expend *jahd* in order to practice *ijtihād*, that is, we need to exert our utmost effort in trying to reach the best decisions and derive the best rulings. *Ijtihād* must not simply be one the basics of the foundation of *shari'ah*. *Ijtihād* must be applied in every aspect of life.

The main reason why there is not a single successful, evident, living Muslim community alive now as an alternative to the *kufr* one is because we have failed in our *Ijtihād*. We have not done enough *Ijtihād* regarding the economic system, the way of life, the trading system, and the monetary system. That is why we are now in the situation of having great scholars but who are confined to basics of *shari'ah*. At the end of the day most of the *'ulamā'* we have cannot deviate from the original structures. They cannot, therefore, come up with anything new in the way of life guidance. Most of the time we are reacting to the change in life that is coming from the West, rather than living a model based on the full path of Islam. We have not developed an economic system as an alternative to the purely secular and materialistic systems. The whole world now is following the modern Western way without any serious ideological or spiritual grafting. We also blindly follow their education systems, sports, entertainments and so forth without being able to add anything meaningful to the content. That is why Muslims find themselves in greater and greater difficulty. At heart we are together, yearning for a way out to revive the Muslims, but in reality, historically and currently we can only show bankruptcy on the social and political side.

On the personal side, however, there is always hope for transformation. At all times every one of us can discover the truth in our hearts and yearn for the light that is already within, above, before and after. The Muslim at all times can save himself on an individual level, but on a community or political level this is another issue.

Muslim communities are also struggling to establish a certain measure of integrity and nobility, which is not easy nowadays because the avalanche of the materialistic secular system is sweeping them aside until they re-establish themselves. We do not know what will happen next. Reviving Muslims implies bringing back to life in a community way which individuals know is right. The individual Muslim knows what is *harām* (out of bounds, forbidden), or what is going to lead him down a slippery path ending in a valley out of which he may not be able to climb. Allah says: *'We have created you from one self...'* [6:98]. We are one person, one reality.

This is why the Prophet was sent as *Rahmatan li'l-'ālamīn*, a Mercy for all mankind. Mankind is one. We are all the children of Adam. The messengers and the prophets came at different times and from different cultures, but there is only one book and one author. Wherever you turn is the trace of that author. Where is it that Allah is not in it, before it and after it? Our differences are superficial. We all have the same questions about life – Is it the right time? Where and how should we proceed? Is this the right job to do or not? Is this the right education? – Our differences are minor. We all would agree that death is the only certainty we can talk about from the time we are born until the time we die. Are we ready for it? Are we ready to admit that we have nothing of our own? We are Allah's guests. *Rahmah* is everywhere, individually and collectively and in other ways. We have to have high expectations of Allah's *rahmah*.

Allah is as good as we expect of Him. If we expect a light and illumination and a correct map to guide us not to deviate, we will have it. If we argue and create dissension and agitation and dispute about this *madhhab* and that *madhhab*, Allah will also give us that. Allah's *rahmah* is wide and deep. If we want to be content in our hearts and share the delight of that light in us, Allah will give us the opportunity to share it. It will overflow. We are accountable to ourselves.

The human being is aware of himself. Life is all about constant awareness! It's all degrees of awareness until such time that we become divinely aware, which is called the *hadrat ar-rabbaniyyah* (Divine Presence). That is why in our *salāt* amongst the subtle conditions is *hudūr ul-qalb* (presence of heart). We first do our *wudu'* (ablution). Next we ascertain where our *qiblah* (direction) is, where our *masjid* (place of worship) is, where we are putting our heads and who is our *Imam*, until our hearts are totally and utterly *bayn 'asabi' ar-rahmān* (between the fingers of the Merciful). We lean on the *Rahmān* to tell us how to change, how to turn the *qalb* (heart). *Qalb* is from the verb *qaliba, yaqlibu* – meaning to turn, that is, you are not fixed. You are light!

Essentially the human being is a *rūh*. The *rūh* illumines the *nafs*. The *nafs* must obey the *rūh* until it knows fully, because Allah says that all of the *arwāh* have been exposed to: *'alastū bi-rabbikum'* (Am I not your Lord?). So we know that Allah knows. Allah will tell us what we need to know at the time we need to know it. Many a time Allah's *rahmah* is such that He keeps us in ignorance. If we knew what was going to come to us in the next four days or all the turmoil, we may die of a heart attack. If we trust in Allah we will see nothing other than endless and utter joy. Then we become *'Abd Allah*.

So as to revive the Muslim, Allah ultimately reminds us: *'O you who believe! Answer (the call of) Allah and His Messenger when he calls you to that which gives you life; and know that Allah intervenes between man and his heart, and that to Him you shall be gathered'* [8:24]. It implies that our life now is biological, physiological, but not illumined. We are not overwhelmed by the joy of the knowledge that Allah knows and that we don't know, but He will give us what we need to know at the time that it is appropriate for us to know; that Allah's *rahmah* will come between us and ourselves because we may be running away here. This is the action of our self. Our hearts told us to go there. Allah teaches us that if you are truly *'abd Allah*, Allah will suddenly change your hearts. Thus your *īmān* in Allah increases and by that *īmān* you will be illumined.

Revival will only come if there is the right quality of Muslims living their *dīn*, consulting each other about how to cope with the difficult circumstances and then the *ummah* will rise. Otherwise, it will remain in a nostalgic daydream or some sort of an expectation which may not necessarily be realized.

Charity begins at home. If we are truly Muslims, then we have to live our *dīn* so others will see us enjoying our path. They will say: 'Please come and show me the atlas. Show me your map. I am constantly having mishaps in my life. Every day I choose a new partner and it is not good. Every time I change my family it is not good. Show me the map so that I don't constantly experience disaster.' The map is the *Qur'ān* and the prophetic way and its application. So many of us think we know because '*Al-hamdulillah*, I am a Muslim,' or because we listen to the *Qur'ān* every day, or 'I am a *Qari* or *Hafiz*.' We may be *hāfiz al-Qur'ān* (memorizer of *Qur'ān*) but has *hifz ul-Qur'ān* (memorization of the *Qur'ān*) given us His *hifz* (protection)? Are we protected by it? There is a big difference between the two states.

We have to have '*azm* (steadfastness) and follow the prophet's *ulū'l-'azm* and know that the lower self has no '*azm* and the *rūh* has no beginning and no end. Follow the direction of the *rūh* and then you will experience *rūhun wa rayhān* (mercy and sweet solace). It becomes a perfume that our Prophet loved. If we stay with the people of perfume and the people of goodness, we will find goodness even in the midst of the most difficult situations which we may be experiencing collectively. And we should not curse *dahr* (time) because *dahr* is Allah. We are exhorted not to curse time. Allah has made it difficult so that it becomes easy to wake up, ready to leave this world in full *jihād*, exercising first our inner *jihād*, and then be with the people whom we love. These things are part of our *jihād* until we understand the full meaning of exerting energy, which does not belong to us in the first place.

We should thank Allah all the time so that when we truly declare *al-hamdu li'llah* we mean it: 'All praise belongs to Allah.' We yearn for Allah's perfect qualities and that is *'ibādah* (worship), which is on a road that is *muhabbah* (love). Clarity brings ease. So for the *'abd Allah* in *'ibādah*, asking Allah's *rahmah* is the only recourse he has. It is called *silāh al-mu'min* (weapon of the believer). The weapon of the believer is to call upon Allah. If someone has a cell-phone and has not paid his subscription or does not know the number he is trying to call, there will be no answer. The attempt to call will be a mockery. We must call upon Allah when we are truly *'abd Allah*, truly trusting in Allah, and knowing there is none other than Allah.

The path to being illumined by Allah is one of submission. Submit to the truth that we have come here into this world to die.

3: THE GLOBAL THIRST FOR INNER AWAKENING

All human beings, irrespective of race, culture or religion, yearn for wellbeing and goodness in life. Spiritual awakening shows that it is sacred grace which is the true essence and source of the universe.

Seekers are people who are observant, who are concerned about meanings and purposes, who want to know the meaning behind this life, who search for the truth, who are on the path of knowledge, and who want to know the solution to the ever-recurring problems that we human beings are constantly faced with.

We are the people who seek this knowledge. We are certain that we will come to know the higher meaning and the purpose of this existence. Equally there are many, many others who have no concern other than their pleasures – short-term pleasures, quick acquisitions, big impositions, immediate power and all the other things that go with the luster of *dunya* (this world). The way of this *dunya* is that it is attractive because it has in it good things, beauties, comforts, wonderful rhythms and harmonies.

A person who is reasonably healthy enjoys all these pleasures, but we all know that none of them can last. Equally we know that we cannot have enough of them. We become greedy, forgetful, selfish and all the other lower qualities, so that the self hardens. Allah reminds us of the truth behind this existence, telling us that '*We created mankind from one self,*' [4:1] that is, from one pattern, one type of *fitrah* (innate nature). Allah also reveals to us:

'I swear by time, Mankind is in a state of loss.' [103:1] At all times, in all civilizations, in all eras, and all cultures throughout history mankind retains his Adamic pattern or Adamic profile. One of the meanings of the word *insān* (man) is that he seeks solace, comfort and reassurance, from *anisa*, to be sociable.

Another derivative of this word can simply mean or imply forgetfulness, because we do forget. We forget that we may leave this world any minute. We forget that we may leave this house and never return. We forget that we are going after something that we want yet it may be our poison. We are forgetful, but is that all we are? Are we only impatient?

Allah also reminds us how magnificent is His Adamic creation because it contains the *rūh*. The Arabic word *rūh* is related to another word which means perfume. From the same root comes *rayhān* (fragrant basil or solace) and also *rīh*, which is wind or breeze. Allah tells us that the make-up of the human being is that there is something divine in us and there is within that, something sublime, which we are yearning for. The *rūh*, that divine inspiration, that spark from Allah is such that it cannot put up with the ever-changing world, the ever demanding material world, with its constrictions, quarrels, discrepancies and disharmonies.

Within the human being, within each one of us, there is an element that yearns for the eternal garden, for *haqq* (absolute truth); yet we are caught in this body, having to relate to the world outside through our senses, having to make some sense out of it with great effort. Every minute you and I are expending energy. If our *jihād* is for the right thing, outer and inner, then our struggle is right. This is according to how Allah designed it. If our *jihād* is for more accumulation of this world, then equally we will suffer because there is no end to it. More of 'this' requires more of 'that'. It never ends.

It is for this reason Allah reveals to us that the normal situation for the average human being is that they are at a loss or in loss. In the end, even if you have accumulated unimaginable wealth, even if you have succeeded in everything, you are going to leave it. That is the final loss. You will depart. So at all times, in every situation, the ordinary situation on the human side is that we will never get the upper hand. Allah has the upper hand. You and I at all times, as normal human beings, are at a loss.

Is that the whole story, however? Allah tells us that it is not: '... Except for those who have faith (that there is a purpose in this life) and do good works' [103:2-3]. The purpose is to worship Him. The word for worship derives from 'abbada, to make smooth or easy. To worship is easy. And the practice of worship generates a deep sense of ease within us. We are created and designed to adore, to be in love with and to worship Allah. That worship is not just in abstract ways or just the occasional recitation of Qur'ān and salāt (ritual prayer). It is a continuous condition and orientation, because Allah describes true worshipers as those in a perpetual state of connectedness or salat [70:23]. The story is completed with 'amilu 's-salihat (and do good deeds), i.e. action, action, action.

The Prophet reminds us that when we die, nothing remains from us except right actions. When we are resurrected we will be resurrected according to our actions and those actions are as good as our intentions were. Faith alone without 'amal (action) is not enough. Having faith that Allah will guide me is only half the story. The picture will not be complete unless I do my best to know Allah, to know His ways, His attributes, His injunctions, His shari'ah and His Prophets; to try and be as if we are surrounded by them, to live as though we are true and worthy followers of the prophet Muhammad. We need to have faith that Allah will guide us and take us out of this world at the right time and that this energy we have, that this life we have, is not ours. It is bought, so we need to do our best.

☼   'Allah does not impose upon any soul a duty but to the extent of its [utmost] ability.' [2:286]

Allah expects from us the limit of our effort. But what is the utmost limit of what we can do? Like a string, it can be long or short according to our perception. The more we can do, the more we find Allah will give us the energy to do it.

The situation in European social systems is crescendoing to a peak, especially in the more so-called developed countries. In Britain the situation for the average human being is so tight that there is not an iota of joy left in it. Daily life often amounts to nothing other than chasing to pay bills. Cities like London are completely blocked up with endless traffic. Mobility is restricted. There is a heavy lid on people's lives. Allah does that for us collectively because we have taken this rational business – more efficiency, more money, more accumulation, better housing – to such an extreme that every house is beautiful but the people living in it are dead.

This is the natural conclusion of collectively misleading ourselves. Yet things are not as dead as they may seem; there is steam building up under the pressure cooker. I have found people are now far more alert to discovering that they are undernourished spiritually. How do we nourish ourselves spiritually? By switching off our minds from the outer world, switching on our hearts into our inner world to know that Allah was, Allah is, and Allah will be and the purpose of all this existence is for us to know that Allah's generosity, His might, power, beauty, majesty, is providing for all including his enemies – *Ar-Razāq* (the Provider); *al-Wahāb* (the Giver), *As-Sabūr* (the Patient) and *al-Halim* (the Forbearantly Clement).

We see many of these attributes in the mother when she greets her child because she is inculcating these attributes of Allah in the child. She is forever available and near – Allah is the ever near.

He says, 'We are closer to him than [his] jugular vein' [50:16]. So whenever there is a lot of constriction and tension, there is also the possibility of release. Life cannot exist without tension. Life in fact exists because of stress. If we are stressed then we start pushing. This gives us the impetus to figure things out: What are we doing? What will we do tomorrow? Are we ready for death? Have we lived this life so that we are aware of what comes next?

Allah tells us: 'And whoever is blind in this, he shall (also) be blind in the hereafter; and more astray from the way' [17:72]. This refers to the world of the subtle energies, in the angelic world, in the world where the physical ability to manipulate no longer is possible. We are all forms with meanings; we are all a mixture of divine light and animal tendencies; we have it all. It depends which side of this spectrum you and I are being tuned to. We can be worse than animals or higher than the angels. This is the spectrum. The tuning dial cannot turn except by 'amal ('āmal as-sālihan) – better action.

Questions that will lead us to better action are: What are you doing to purify yourself? What are you doing to serve others who are less fortunate than you? Better action, improved intention with no expectation, is freeing. What drive us are expectations, desires, lust and fears. Fear is the cause of all constrictions. Allah tells us in the Qur'ān that there is no possibility of life except as one of two, both forms as well as meanings: if there is good, there is evil. You cannot have one without the other. One leads to the other and comes from the other. All the nafs wants is expansion and sometimes expansion is its worst disease.

Constriction is the answer – no possibility of choice. If we do not know what to do, we should stay where we are. What is the mihrab (prayer niche) other than no choice? What is the qiblah (direction of prayer) other than no choice? Here you have no choice other than giving up to Allah. The salvation for a community lies in realizing that the self has these lower tendencies, but that also within it lies the *rūh*, this amazing means to aspire to the higher and be guided by the *rūh*, through the heart, through the *qalb*. The word *qalaba* means to turn away, to change – we must constantly change what we thought was important, so it loses its importance. We may think something is important, but if we are ready to die we will find it to be of no great importance. We are all leaving after all, and nothing can come with us.

We need to be constantly doing the right action as though doing it for the last time in life and reminding each other of the truth. The definition of *'aql* in our heritage in our *dīn* is intellect. It is that power or faculty that moves you towards the truth. The truth is that which never changes. Values will never change. The values of our great prophets will never change. They all said the same thing. The essence of these messages are the same. The truth never ever changes but there are relative realities, for example, sickness is real, but that state will change. Our desire for equilibrium and peace never changes. Peace is one of Allah's names – *as-Salām* – and that quality never alters, just as *al-Haqq* (the Truth) never changes. We are all aspiring for the *Haqq*. *Haqq* is absolute truth. All other realities are relative to this.

Therefore what we are actually yearning for is the knowledge that Allah is there for us, with us and all we need is to turn to Him. Allah is ever-available but are we available? Where is it that Allah is not? Allah says: '*And be patient, for surely Allah does not waste the reward of the doers of good*' [11:115].

There were messengers and prophets who did not have more than their own household follow them. The Prophet reminds us in a great tradition that: 'A time will come when it will be difficult for man to uphold his religion, and to save it he will flee from one cave to another cave and from one hillock to another, like the jackal with its offspring escaping tyranny.' He was asked when that would be, to which he replied, 'At that time when everybody will be pushing to earn his keep through illicit ways, through *harām* (unlawful, usurious) ways, when one will be ruined by the hand of one's parents, and if he has no parents, then at the hands of his wife and children, and in their absence, at the hands of relatives.' People were shocked to hear this for their assumption was that family and marriage is so important in our *dīn*.

Our times are difficult. We must accept it. We must realize what is happening. We must realize the stranglehold the techno-usurious practices hold over the world. We must realize how our ways of life have been shattered. Everyone is for themselves in small houses. We must realize that the human links in our community are weak and the help we give each other is at a minimum. Everybody is running to the bank for help. We must realize our weakness and then ask Allah for strength. Then we must do something about it; otherwise it will remain a mixture of fantasy, anger, disappointment and also a lot of talk that will last until we stop talking.

Our *dīn* is based on listening and hearing, understanding it in our *fitrah* (primordial state), in our heart and then acting upon the insight given. Al-Muhāsibi, one of the greatest philosopher-theologian masters (d.857 CE), said that *ma'rifah* (gnosis or inner knowledge) is based on four things: First – *Ma'rifatu 'llah*: knowing Allah's ways and that His ways will never change – 'As you are, thus will you be ruled.' If we do not change, nothing will change. How do we change? Stop and change our minds. If something is important to us, in a few minutes it may no longer be important. Make something else more important. We may have thought our son was the most important thing. He may turn out to be the worst for us. He may be our worst enemy. Find people whom our hearts can go for, and serve and help them. Nowadays, we are living in situations where our homes are constricting – we may have 2 or 3 bedrooms only. We cannot suddenly have a lot of people there, but what about our workplace? Why can't we open up our workplace for us to see our other brothers, who are not brothers by blood, but by heart, by love, and by affection? This is the way of the Prophet. We cannot improve on it. This is the way of his family, of his brothers and of his friends. We cannot improve on these things.

The time we are living in has its difficulties, but it also has its ease. We must travel in the land more frequently to find out who we are, who our other brothers and sisters are. They may not be next door to us. At the time when travel was restricted in every town and city, there were people of *'ilm* and knowledge in one area, and in another people of commerce, and in yet another worthy artisans. Now we may have to travel far to find our brothers, but it's easier nowadays than ever before. Let us not curse the times we live in. We have to comprehend the situation, the time we are living in, and then live and maintain values according to modern times.

A second thing al-Muhāsibi says is that the key to *'irfān* (gnosis) is knowledge of the self, to know that the self is treacherous – *'Man is at all times in a state of loss.'* We know that we are created so that we see the limitations of the self, its meanness and impatience. We therefore call upon Allah to cover us: *Astaghfiru'llah* – 'I ask Allah to cover me.' I see my impatience, so I ask Allah who is the Ever-Patient – *As-Sabūr* – to cover me. I see my impertinence, my constant defense of myself, so I ask Allah to cover me with his *rahmah* (mercy), with His attributes, with His *jalāl* (majesty) and with His *jamāl* (beauty*)*.

Once we know ourselves, we are on the way to knowing our Lord. *'Whoever knows himself, then knows his Lord,'* i.e. knows how to put the self aside which allows the *nur* that is always there to beam. You have to transcend the self, knowing that it is always there, without justifying.

It is of no use to blame everybody else except the self. We may feel a bit better, but it is not going to help us along in our spiritual progress. Ultimately that is based on *'ibadah* (worship). How can we worship Allah unless we know Allah's ways, Allah's attributes and Allah's commands? Unless we know the way of the Prophet that leads us to that courtyard of saving ourselves from ourselves by Allah's *rahmah*? We need knowledge of Allah, knowledge of self, then thirdly, according to *al-Muhasibi*, knowledge of the *dunyā* – how the world works. This is clear for us in the *Qur'ān* and in the way of Allah and in the way of the Prophet. If we don't know, we should ask those who know better. Is it the right time? Is it the right place? The nature of *dunyā* is that it appears to be soft, but it is like being bitten by a snake: once we are close and are poisoned by money-making and usury, we have had it.

Lastly, the most important thing to avoid is *Shaytān* and the multitudes of *shaytanic* ways. Our *dīn* is nothing other than living this life inwardly full of joy, inwardly full of contentment, inwardly overflowing with the knowledge of Allah's *rahmah*, while outwardly doing what we can and struggling in the way of Allah. Struggling will never stop no matter whether the being is a prophet, a messenger, or the greatest *walī* (friend of Allah or saint) on earth. Outer afflictions will continue, irrespective of the person, but if the inner is balancing the outer, then it is easier.

The prophets and the messengers have had more afflictions and more outer trouble than any other human beings. But once their inner is in balance, they know it is Allah's way; and though they know that human beings are mischievous, they also know that Allah decrees *rahmah*. We have to be very aware of the cosmology of the individual and society in this time and age and also to be careful of afflicting others as this will not only affect the perpetrators and those who are creating these *fitnahs* and troubles, but will afflict everybody. It is not only I who will suffer if I set fire to my house: the next-door neighbor and the whole neighborhood will suffer. That's why the Muslim has to be alert and vigilant, and that is why we cannot say that it does not concern us. If it does not concern you now, it will concern you soon.

I will never forget what my brother, Shaykh Asaf's, once said during an earth-shattering talk in England. When the trouble in Bosnia began. He said, *'You people in England are sitting cozy now. You say it does not matter to you what is happening in Bosnia, but look at the misery of millions of people there. Look at what is going on. You talk about human rights but see what they are doing to the innocent women. It will come to you. Watch out. It will come to you. You cannot say I do not have anything to do with it. You have to be concerned.'* This is the quality of the Prophet: concern for people. You cannot say simply that they are *kuffar*. The *kuffar* are perpetrators of *kufr* but they are also suffering.

Our first priority goes to those who are close to us – our families, our friends – but equally it must be *'rahmatan li'l-'ālamīn'* (a mercy for all mankind). If we are truly plugged into the divine light, and if you are illumined within, you are content with Allah's ways and discontent with the outer. If you are doing your best cheerfully, I guarantee you that other people will want to be with you. We are all in the same situation: everybody is suffering and confused. It is only the *mu'min* who is in *jihād*, who is doing his or her best, who is also maintaining outward boundaries. Inwardly they always have ease. Outwardly they know the world is both ease and difficulty. You cannot have one without the other. Allah says: *'Verily with every difficulty there is ease. Verily, with every difficulty there is ease'* [94:5-6].

You cannot exclude fear and therefore we need to constrict fears. If you fear Allah, then you have no other fear. If you do not fear Allah, then you will have every other fear, starting with the bank manager and ending up with all kinds of other fantasy fears. Fear is ignorance of Allah. This is because we are not doing our *'ibadah* (worship) properly. We are not ready to leave this world.

These are the key issues. These are the transformative issues we need to focus on, otherwise we grow more and more informed and less and less transformed, less and less living life, more and more reading about it. What matters is *your* life. Are you ready to leave it? If you are ready to leave it, then you are reasonably qualified to deal with it and that can only come when we acknowledge our ignorance, when we know we are in a state of loss and we plead to Allah to cover us and our ignorance and to guide us as to where we get information, where we get knowledge and for us to remain courteous. *Adab* (courtesy) to Allah is to be as though you do not exist, as in *sajdah* (prostration). In *sajdah* your profile is obliterated. *Adab* towards creation is to see their trouble, to see what is afflicting them, so that they begin to see that Allah's *rahmah* is there. If all of us get what we want, the world will fall to billions of pieces. There is a tyrant latent in every one of us.

The Prophet says, 'If you want to satisfy the greed of one person, you could not satisfy it by filling up the biggest valleys with gold.' Therefore, be people of the garden. In the garden there is everything and beyond, so there is no need. Here we are imprisoned in this body for a while until we realize that the jailer is Allah. We were sent down to earth so that we could realize that our origin belongs to a zone of truth and never-changing magnificence: paradise. This life is only for a short period. We try our best to prepare for the ultimate garden and save ourselves from *shaytanic* tendencies, keeping quiet under the protection of Allah's *Rahmanic* tendencies and *Rahmanic* intentions and constantly remembering the way of the Prophet and living as though he is with us, living as though we are worthy of him and then helping each other. Then the whole world will be glorify in a way that we understand.

Allah says: '*Whatsoever is in the heavens and whatsoever is on the earth glorifies Allah*' [59:1]. We are all yearning for the divine names. We all possess an aspect of the *al-Ghani*, the source of all wealth, of *al-Qawwi*, the source of power, of *al-Baqi*, the source of everlastingness, of *al- Awwal, al-Akhir* and so on. These are the ways that the heart comes to life and if the heart is alive, then the rest is alright. You can then deal with life.

> *Allah is ever available but are we available?*
> *Where is it that Allah is not?*

4: URGENT DUTIES OF A MUSLIM

*Constant awareness and personal responsibility for all
thoughts, intentions and actions will lead to higher states of
consciousness and awareness of the sacredness of life.*

I would like to share with you today a very important concern which
is to do with our life, our journey, and discovery of the truth and
worship (*ibādah*). This is to do with the continuous urgency for us to
perform our duties and therefore we need to define, or dwell upon,
the meaning of the word urgency, the meaning of time and of duty.
If we are to truly revive our hearts and our way of life (*dīn*), then we
need to first grasp the meanings and the directions of the map of
existence and follow it.

With this map you realize you are in the divine city. The *Qur'ān*
relates to us how Allah's voice came to Prophet Musa (a.s.) and tells
him to take off his shoes, i.e. his protection and presumptions, for
he was already in the divine valley. Where is it that Allah is not? The
earth and the heavens are His. The air and birds are His. You are
His. Remembering this brings about that urgency, that immediacy
of higher awareness. As Muslims we have been endowed with this
tremendous heritage of the *Qur'ān*, the way and the history (*sīrah*) of
Muhammad. When these teachings are lived they are transformative.

Unless we delve into our heritage and imbibe it, we will remain
Muslims in name only, that is, pseudo-Muslims who have not been
transformed and illumined. You will find in the *Qur'ān* hundreds
of verses to do with knowledge (*'ilm*) – well over 800 or 900 *ayāt*

and about half of them mentioned knowledge along with action (*'amal*); they go together. These are the foundations of duty. What is your duty, to what and when? And how can one duty become more important than the other, because you and I are living entities. We are not machines nor are we mechanical. You may have a duty towards your family: you are taking your groceries back home when suddenly you see a blind person crossing the road. You can see that the traffic is very heavy. Inevitably he or she is going to be run over. So you abandon your first duty of rushing home with your groceries to help this person to cross the road. What happened? How did this priority change? It is basically that you saw yourself as the same self as any other human being: *'He created you from one self and from it its pair'* [39:6]. On some level you realized the other person is potentially the same as you. You have sympathy, compassion and this short-lived duty of helping this person to cross the road will only take a bit of your time and then you return to your old habit of caring for the immediate family. There is a constant hierarchy and change of duties.

Now the question of time (*'asr* or *waqt*) is another key issue. If you do not experience it fully, within yourself, then you will remain unfulfilled. Time is Allah's indicator, which He has given to the children of Adam to realize that originally we are from no time, from non-time, from the eternal garden. There are many verses in the *Qur'ān* that allude to this. He says: *'There surely came over man a period of time when he was a thing not worth mentioning'* [76:1].

This is Allah's laboratory or kindergarten, one which is based on time and space. Originally we are a *rūh* that is from before time and space. It is being caught in this prison of time and space for us to realize the perfection of Allah's lights. Wherever you look is an aspect of His light. We need to realize that Allah's lights and His perfections are what we are always seeking so that we are ready to return to the garden of eternity where there is no time but only perfection. Allah has designed it so that we are caught in this constant change, good to bad, up and down, breathing in, and out, shadows that never stop so that we appeal to the highest within us as a reference point. In that way we can make sense out of nonsense.

This is called remembrance of Allah (*dhikru'llah*). We have to perform the perfect rituals and ways of our glorious Prophet. Allah says: '*...surely prayer keeps (one) away from shameful and evil deeds, and certainly the remembrance of Allah is the greatest, and Allah knows what you do.*' [29:45].The key here is avoiding the error of indecent and unjust ways; this is mirrored in the *kalima*: *la ilāha* – 'no other' – and *illa'llah* – 'except Allah'. The remembrance (*dhikr*) of Allah is everywhere. How can we ever forget that which is the source of remembrance and forgetfulness? It is pre-memory. The knowledge of Allah, the light of Allah, was before any patterns of existence. Allah reminds us in the *Qur'ān* in so many ways of the urgency, the importance of the moment. If you miss the moment, you probably have missed a lifetime.

Reflect on the meaning of these few verses of the *Qur'ān*.

☼   '...but We leave those alone who hope not for Our meeting in their trespasses, wandering on distractedly.' [10:11]

And:

☼   'There comes not to them a new reminder from their Lord but they hear it while they sport.' [21:2]

An interesting word in Arabic is *la'ab* (play or sport), which implies distraction. In Arabic these words of playing or sport are akin to *salwa* (entertainment). *Tasliyah* means to be distracted from the truth. Amazingly the original meaning of 'sport' or entertainment is to be distracted from the truth. The truth is so great, so effulgent, of such high voltage that you cannot take it, so you start fooling around. Allah tells us that awareness comes to us constantly; the implicit knowledge that there is only Allah is continuously renewed. There is only the One source of every plurality or of every opposite, but we cannot absorb this fully. Allah says: *They see it (the reckoning) as far, but we see it near'* [70:6-7].

Those of you who are health orientated, you know that if you have a negative thought it will register in you and make you ill. Illness is only a reflection of your wrong attitudes, wrong thinking, wrong habits and wrong life style. Allah in His mercy (*rahmah*) gives us these mirrors continuously to realize what is basically wrong. What is fundamentally wrong is that we are not performing our *'ibādah* perfectly. How can we perform our *'ibādah* perfectly unless we have an understanding of Allah's ways and Allah's patterns and what is acceptable to Allah and what is not, so that we always see the perfect light behind what appears to be confusion?

There are so many occasions in our lives that we are not happy with what has happened to our destiny, but if we stop and look back with the higher light in us, we will see it was perfect. You placed your foot wrongly, you thought wrongly, and you deserved the consequence. The suffering is Allah's mercy (*rahmah*) to show you that if you do not see perfection within every instant and every situation, then your worship (*'ibādah*) is not fulfilled. You are not holding on to the rope of Allah (*hablu'llah*). Being connected to the rope of Allah does not mean you will never experience injustice. Nor does it mean you do not recognize that things outwardly are out of balance. You do. But you equally see the message behind it. You also see what Allah is showing you. Collectively we have sunk into abuse, into the love of materialism (*dunya*), into forgetfulness, into the lack of readiness for departure. Ultimately the urgency lies in our willingness to depart.

The trick of time is that you and I function in time, but our *rūh* is from non-time. We are both eternal and ephemeral. The body will have to be returned because it is borrowed. The *rūh* and the *nafs* will continue. This is the model we have. If we as Muslims do not live it fully then we are not worthy of our heritage. We will miss the thrill of illumination and delight. If we are not delighted, then we have missed the message that Allah was, Allah is, Allah will be, Allah is before you, Allah is after you and you have been created in order to know Him, love Him, and adore Him. If this is not the ultimate glorious gift, I do not know what is.

In our teachings time is taken seriously. The Prophet said of it: *'Time is like a sword, if you do not cut it, it will cut you'*. When you hear people say 'next time', 'next year ', especially with *'inshallah'*, it will never happen. The essence of what the Prophet was alluding to is, for example, when you do your ablutions *(wudu)*, you are sealing yourself from outside distractions. When you say, 'In the name of Allah' *(Bismillah)* you plunge into worship for your own sake so that you are led by the highest in you, which is your soul *(rūh)*. It is often quoted that Imam Ali (a.s.) said: *'Work in this world as though you are going to live forever...'* It means that we should postpone worldly things. If you need a new car, don't rush for it. Wait for the next few days. Leave your worldly affairs, for they do not matter. Postpone them. The second half of that saying is, *'And work for your next life as though you are going to die tomorrow.'* Consider that every moment is the last hour. With this outlook whatever you say will be real. Whatever you think of is focused. Your state is infinite now because the minute is infinite.

Descriptions of duty are extensively described in our teachings: *'There is not a moment without some duty'*; and *'Do the duty that is nearest to you and the next one becomes clearer to you'*. Negligence of duty will obscure the truth for you. We neglect it because we are selective. Allah has given us a challenge; ask Him to help you to deal with the challenge. Also, problems cannot always be resolved. But if we are willing to face them, they will dissolve. Whenever the problem arises, the solution is there. Be the servant of Allah *('abd Allah)*. Be helpless in yourself and hopeful by Him. And then you find creation is alright. You will find that everybody is fumbling about, doing their best, some of them without a map or a direction. Others think they have a direction and a map yet are fumbling even worse.

Practice what you know and what you don't know will become clearer to you. It is knowledge and action ('*ilm wa 'amal*). These two go together. Act upon that which you know and what you don't know will become clearer to you. Then the next action will unveil for you even more. Be honest. Be correct. Be ready to leave it all because you never had it all anyway.

We should be practicing higher consciousness all the time. Allah tells us through his revelations that the entire business of the *dīn* is based on 'those who believe in the unseen.' We believe in the unseen. The dream is closer to the truth than this world. What does this mean? This world is solid. The dream is more subtle. The seen world is merely the tip of the iceberg. There are countless trillions of energies and entities of angels and others that we do not know. So it is not just a question of belief in the unseen. We know that the unseen prevails over the seen – I am temporarily here in the cage of the body in the seen. Eventually we will leave it behind, and we yearn for the unseen.

In addition to urgency, there is also patience (*sabr*). There are so many beautiful verses in the *Qur'ān* about *sabr* – Allah's name is *As-Sabur* (the Patient). Allah addresses the Prophet and therefore us: '*Have patience the same way as the great ones had, those who had constant, persistent determination – the great Prophets.*' Generally and traditionally we have been told that these are the five great prophets: Ibrahim, Mūsa, Nuh, Isa and Muhammad (*peace be upon them all*).

They were people who were determined. For 950 years the prophet of Allah Nuh (a.s.) was repeating the message: '*O people, you will bring upon yourself catastrophic events by your actions*'. He could hear the rumblings of the earth, the abuse of the environment, as we are doing now. We have hardly left anything in this world unpolluted – the seas, the skies and everywhere you look has been poisoned by our interference. The Prophet Nuh (a.s.) was saying the same thing; he tried to warn hi people to stop and change direction because he knew they would be doomed, until, at the end Allah's inspiration came to him to save himself and the representatives of creation and they floated away in the ark until the flood subsided.

Another verse says: *These shall be granted their reward twice, because they are steadfast and they repel evil with good and spend out of what We have given them* [28:54]. Contemplate this verse and the word 'twice'. Look at Allah's mercy. Once is when you have stopped impatience, you then begin to see things as they are. One of the greatest prophetic *du'ās* (supplication) is: *'Oh, Allah, show me things as they are'*, i.e. not colored by my own biography and by my own expectations. You must have expectations, but do not be colored by them. Put them aside every now and then. Take the colored lens out of your eye. See things as they are.

There is an avalanche now overwhelming the world – an avalanche of love and worship of this world, the *dunya*. Pollution abounds everywhere. This is the time we are living in. If you do not see it, you are misleading yourself. You must see how poisoned everybody is, over-drugged by allopathic and legalized drugs whose side-effects are far worse than their supposed benefits. If you don't see things as they are, then you are living in a fantasy and we are just preaching into thin air. We will not get anywhere. That is why if there is going to be a true change and revival in the hearts of Muslims it is going to be by stopping first and taking stock of the patient who is hallucinating. So you get your reward twice once you see things as they are.

This morning before coming here, a friend had called me from Malaysia. He was on his way to England just an hour ago. He was telling me that he had made the biggest mistake by travelling by Gulf

Air because the behavior of some of the Gulf male passengers was so obnoxious that everybody was disturbed during the flight. When they landed he gave them a firm talking to and the staff of the aircraft applauded because they couldn't say much. Because my friend is an Arab and quite well-known and dignified, he was able to rebuke them. I asked him was he now going to teach them to be hypocrites? They were, after all, revealing who they were and now he was telling them to hide it behind a smoke screen. We laughed about it.

Our observations and awareness of those observations must be real. It is no use trying to put on a nice little act when inside you are full of anger, hatred and jealousy. Who are you hiding from? Allah knows. So: be <u>one</u>. If you are not one, how can you talk about the One, let alone come close to know the One. You will indeed get your reward twice. The first reward is being real now. The second is that it will pass, things will change. We are all on our way to the garden. We are here practicing being in the garden by avoiding the fire.

Look at Allah's amazing depth of knowledge that He shines upon us through the *Qur'ān*. A third verse says:

> ☼   'And We will surely test you until We make evident those who strive among you [for the cause of Allah] and the patient, and We will test your affairs.' [47:31]

Meaning: you will be afflicted. You will have problems. Every day, every moment, every hour, you will face a disturbing challenge so that you know who the people in *Jihād* really are. What does *Jihād* mean? It means exerting energy to unveil the truth at all its levels. A true *Mujahid* is exerting energy, as best as he can – by hand, by mouth, by mind, by limbs. This is outer *Jihād*. You are all the time in outer *Jihād*. You are moving your hands, you are moving your limbs, and you are sitting. You are in *Jihād* all the time. *Jihād*, however, must be appropriate to you at the right time. *Jihād* is also silence. It is also having patience. It is a big *jihād* to be patient about things you want which you know are not allowed (*harām*) or allowed (*halāl*) but unattainable in that moment.

Exerting energy to unveil the truth of the difficulties that you find yourself in and being patient in them: this is *Jihād*. If there is nothing you can do for the time being, be patient. Allah wants you to practice patience. It is another form of gymnastics or exercise. Be patient. Be patient for five years. It is not important. Allah continues to say in the verse so that: '*We make evident those who strive among you [for the cause of Allah] and the patient [as-sabirin], and We will test your affairs.*' So it means that patience is greater than all forms of *jihād* that we know – it is the ultimate. But it doesn't mean that we can misuse this to cleverly manipulate knowledge. If there is a time for us to rush out and help, for example, when people are afflicted by floods, and you say now I'm in *sabr*, this is not *sabr*. This is *shaytan*.

We all know what the truth is. You can't fool all the people all the time, although it is sometimes quite near to that when it comes to banking and the financial world. Then the word *islāh* (restoration or correction) is key in relation to *sabr* (patience); along with action (*'amal*) and knowledge (*'ilm*) doing the right action (*islāh*) competes the picture. Sometimes it can be by being silent, sometimes by stopping another person and sometimes by warning others. *Islāh* at other times is giving them the good news that you are Adam's son and Allah has created you for the garden and the design is in you. Just follow the map. Allah speaks of those who act correctly, appropriately, whether male or female in *Iman*, in faith that Allah will guide us: '*Whoever does good whether male or female and he is a believer, We will most certainly make him live a happy life, and We will most certainly give them their reward for the best of what they did*' [16:97]. Allah is with us, Allah is before us, Allah is after us. Allah's mercy and compassion (*rahmah*) encompasses every situation. Then Allah ends the *ayah* saying: '*We will most certainly make him live a happy life, and We will most certainly give them their reward for the best of what they did.'* That means our life now is biological and simple, but real life is to awaken into the eternal light – the light of Allah that is energizing us, which was there before us, within us, that will also take us out of this world, back into the world of no time and no space.

There is an urgency here. If you cannot do it now, when will you do it? This postponement is a *la'ab wa lahuw* – diversion and play from that which is too powerful. Do not delay it. And Allah reminds us in the *Qur'ān: 'Your account is near'*. Whatever thought you have is going to be registered in your cells. It is urgent for your sake. Allah tells us: *'When you do good, you do good for your own souls, and if you do evil, it shall be for them'* [17:7]. Allah does not need the good we do. We need it so that we see His reflections and His lights everywhere so that ultimately His light overflows in our hearts, which is His *'arsh* (throne).

The urgency of appropriate action is upon us all the time and our duty is to truly know that there is none other than Allah. Our duty is to know and live forever by the knowledge that there is none worthy of worship other than Allah. And the reflection of it and the echo on this earth is that Muhammad is His messenger. So that is our duty: to acknowledge the truth, that we have no independence. And our duty is to acknowledge the eternal truth that wherever you turn, an aspect of it hits us. Even falsehood is the reverse side of the truth. Allah has allowed the creation of lies, injustices and falsehood, simply as indicators of what is the opposite. Where is it that Allah's mercy (*rahmah*) is not found? Allah says in the *Qur'ān*:

☼   'To Allah belong the East and the West: whither you turn, thither is Allah's presence; surely Allah is all-Pervading, all-Knowing.' [2:115]

This is the great news as Allah describes it in a *du'a*: *'Our Lord! we believe in what You have revealed and we follow the messenger, so write us down with those who bear witness'* [3:53]. Even in the face of the greatest mess in the world, Allah is in charge.

Allah is allowing us all collectively to suffer so that we find a way out of this cul-de-sac that we have brought upon ourselves in the last 200 or 300 years. We have not lived our *din* fully and the *kufr* system prevailed; it has used and abused the power of the financial institutions backed by the corporate world backed by the policing of politics which is nothing other than simply keeping prisons full and collecting taxes to pay the banks. This is the world we are in. The good news is that the light (*nur*) of Allah will prevail. If you and I see the Light, then we will begin to understand the first years of Makkah, how the Prophet was surrounded by the *kufr* system of that time. So we must be real. We must inwardly be joyful; outwardly we must do our best with consciousness, with conscientiousness, with *hilm* (forbearance), with patience. We need to be accountable. Then we will have performed our duty towards ourselves, towards creation and towards the Creator. They all go together.

Amongst the signs of success at the end is referring to
Allah at the beginning.

5: SELF-KNOWLEDGE IS THE FOUNDATION OF OUR *DĪN*

The Qur'ān is a fountainhead of knowledge. Self awareness and self knowledge unlock many other channels of insights & delights.

The Prophet showed us and those close to him, his family and the other *awliyā* (saints) and enlightened beings that we have no choice: all we need to do is absorb the *Qur'ān*, live the *Qur'ān* and remember the ways of the Prophet. The journey will then take us back to where we belong: the Garden.

☼ '(As for) those who believe and do good, a good final state shall be theirs and a goodly return'. [13:29]

Allah has created us for eternal bliss – *as-saʿādah al-abadiyah*. In Arabic happiness or bliss is *saʿāda*. *Saʿīd* means happy, content, joyful. We have to be prepared for our transition into the next life. By the time the last breath comes if you are not in that state of readiness, a huge shock will be waiting for you in the grave.

Allah has given us the entire foundation of this knowledge in the *Qur'ān*. The age we are living in is such that society and community boundaries and all the other controlling factors have become very loose, if not disappearing. I grew up in a community where you could not turn around without somebody looking at you, encouraging, or discouraging, or in some way monitoring you. Wherever you looked there was a mirror for the self to behave itself so that as you grew you were groomed. Hundreds of such societies existed throughout

Muslim history. In every community in every town or village, everybody was responsible. Thus the self was groomed; the lower self became tethered and controlled.

As time has passed we Muslims have not maintained a strong, on- going society or community ethos; we now have a situation where we practice alien values, an alien way of life, an alien way of thinking, alien education, an alien health system and an alien way of dealing with economic activities – all of it is alien to us. Now we can either be angry, and blame everybody else for this or ask what can we do now? In a very small way, in my own life, I have found that the answers are clear.

Young people nowadays are not worse than young people a hundred years ago. The only difference is that they are subjected to cultural cross-currents that are very different from then. It is not their fault that they are now, as some parents call them, 'disobedient', nasty or disrespectful. A torrent has overtaken hundreds of safe, healthy, well-living communities all over the world.

The answer I can share with you is very simple. Instead of the control mechanism coming from the uncles and the aunts and the cousins and the people in the village or in the community, the control mechanism must now come from within. It must be self-control. It must be self-awareness, self-reprimand, self-correction. We do not have the luxury of having been surrounded by relatives and friends and a community that will remind us when we are behaving insanely. We are doing things that will damage ourselves and conduct ourselves in a way that causes us to punish ourselves: because Allah will not punish us, rather, we will punish ourselves through our own wrong actions. Allah does not punish us because of our wrong actions. He punishes us *through* our wrong actions. So it is all self-built. It is already done, already programmed. Each person must discover that if he does wrong, he wrongs himself – as the *Qur'ān* declares, and as the Prophetic teaching reminds us repeatedly. When a person realizes that if he is going to be nasty and hateful, cheating and lying, he will damage himself, then anyone who loves himself, as all human beings are inclined to do normally, he will correct it. He will realize that he does want to damage himself and will thus self-correct.

The *kitāb* (the *Qur'ān*) and the *sunnah* (the prophetic example) do not change, but the way of enabling people to absorb their teachings and live them needs to change according to the culture that we are living in globally. A hundred years ago, the only way for people to be educated was in the *madrasah*. Fifty years ago, mixed systems with the secular way of teaching, many of which were imported from abroad, and the *madrasah* lingered on. That was during my age as a child. By that time the *madrasah* could not make an impact anymore and a few decades after that, attending them became more or less a sort of sacrifice, enduring simplicity and hardship, reflected as an act of piety, or as a last resort of the poor and disenfranchised. It is not the fault of the *madrasah* or the teacher. It is that times have changed. Another system has been grafted on to whatever culture of education we had: secular education. The reason is because our *madrasahs* did not progress by introducing the teaching of mathematics and geography and physics and other subjects, which the West did eight or nine hundred years ago. It is not the fault of anyone. It is events.

If we do not read the events, then we are not living according to the glorious teaching of our Prophet when he says: '*O Allah, show me things as they are.*' Instead, we will blame everybody and get nowhere. So there is no point in just blaming and accusing others – the *madrasah* or anything or anyone else.

Let us look at the situation as it is. A young person living now in a nuclear type of a family with the two or three bedroom syndrome with parents feeling guilty and trying to bribe the poor child with toys, are not going to make an impact on him, unless he or she realizes that by *salāt* they will get fine-tuned in concentrating their mind, that when they do their *wudu* they are now purifying themselves from past mistakes or bad thoughts, that now they are pure and 'sealed' from the world. In that state of readiness they are now able to communicate with the maker of the world, Allah. Thus, when they go into *sajdah*, they go into another zone of awareness. It is no longer mental. It is post-mind or beyond thought. The practice of *salāt* will enable a young child to be far more focused in their studies, in their conduct and in their university. It is training to be far more present in the moment than being chaotic, which is the case for most children, especially when they are overfed with sweets and sugar.

There are major diseases in the age we are living in but we have the medicine for it. We just have to apply it. Within my lifetime, I have come across many young people who have returned to the *dīn* and enjoyed all of our practises of '*ibādah*, our prayers, our *sawm* (fasting) because they found it had an impact upon their own life. In other words, people come to the *dīn* once they find that they are responsible to themselves. They can cheat their parents, they can lie, but at the end of the day are they better off? So to return people to the morality and the ethics of our *dīn*, the times we are living in are such that they must be given the map of the self – Who are you? Why do you do this? Why are you not doing that? In this way the person realizes that it is for their own sake. Allah says: '*in ahsantum fa-li-anfusikum...,*' If you do goodness it is for your own self and if you do wrong it is against yourself.' You yourself are fully responsible.

This core truth that any good you do, or any practice you engage in that is worshipful and oriented towards higher consciousness, is why I say the age we are living in now can be dealt with, or an individual can remain afloat in this life in spite of the dreadfulness that is overtaking the nation's morality and ethics and in spite of the fact that everything has become more or less based on money and quantity ('how much does it cost?' as against 'what value is it to you in this short journey?'). In spite of all of this, we can deal with it if we are totally aware of ourselves, questioning ourselves and our actions – Why are you doing this? Why are you going there? What is your intention?

When we are doing our *wudu'* we should be aware that we are sealing ourselves from anything 'other ' than total, focused orientation towards the higher, doing the same as the Prophet Isa and John the Baptist did in ancient times. Baptism means immersion in water so that we are purified. Ours is much more frequent. They Jews and Christians do it once in a lifetime. We are doing it all the time. We purify ourselves with this symbolic act of making *wudu'* with water and then entering into a dialogue with Allah and then bowing, having been overcome by His glory, and then prostrating, having been totally overcome by the knowledge that there is only One. So we disappear into our *sajdah*.

I want to share with you the verses in the *Qur'ān* that are to do with the self. The word *nafs* means more than just self. It also means *rūh*. It also means person. Many of our commentators have done a lot of work on this, among them *Imam al-Rāzi* for example, whose *tafsirs* are well-known and available. He categorizes the meaning of the *nafs* in the *Qur'ān* in at least five different categories which work and make sense. One is to do with *insān*, which means the person. So although Allah says *nafs*, He means *insān*, meaning a mixture of soul and an ego. There are a number of verses simply referring to *insān* as well. Here we will just share with you the *ayat* that refer to *nafs* in which it means *insān*.

☼ Allah says: '...and whatever good you send before for yourselves, you shall find it with Allah; surely Allah sees what you do.' [2:110]

In other words, you will find it with Allah. You will find it eternal. '*Li-anfusikum'* here means 'to or for yourself'. Another verse: '*No self will be given more responsibility than it can cope with.'* Again, here it is neither the *rūh* nor the lower self, but the reference is to the whole *insān*. We all know there is a higher self called *rūh*, which is pure and from the command of my Lord (*min amri rabbi*), as well as the lower self which is the egocentricity of the so-called you, I, he and she, which changes every instant, whereas the *rūh* is ever constant. It has in it the imprint of the divine knowledge.

☼   And then: '...and no self knows in what land they shall die; surely Allah is Knowing, Aware.' [31:34]

So again, He is talking about *insān* because the *insān* will experience death. And yet we all know that after this death there is an on-goingness. What we have done by ourselves and our *rūh* continues after we have left the body. So we have the cosmology of who we are and what we can be. Once we have this map, and we know that there are keys to this map, we need to read it appropriately. What is the use of having a map of Johannesburg if you cannot read whether this line means a road that has come to an end or a river? Often we look at a river, which is blue, and we think that this is a nice road. It is not a road. So: we need to know the keys to the map.

These are our teachings. This is the *dīn*. To know the *dīn* means to know how to live a way of life. It means 'life's transaction' and how to read aspects of life's existence so that we can then have a relatively safe journey. Just as the map of Johannesburg has in it details and descriptions which need to be interpreted, so too does our *Qur'ān* need to be read, interpreted, and internalized.

Then we want to travel. Travelling along the roads of life implies having first obtained a license, having mastered the highway code. The *Sunnah* of the Prophet is this highway code because his conduct during the journey of life was perfect. Therefore, you and I who do not want to bump into or be bumped by others, need not only a proper license – having practiced enough in the first instance – but also have the right role model. That is the meaning of having love of the Prophet.

So we have the map, the atlas, the keys, the driving license and a good car. It is still not enough. What if there is a huge traffic jam so that we are not going to be able to move along the road? The journey may take six hours instead of two. Somebody called me the day before yesterday from England congratulating me on having left Britain if for no other reason than the traffic jams! Living in central London, he had to take his sick mother to a hospital about five kilometers away; the journey took two hours going and another two hours to return. There is gridlock.

We know the map. We have the car and the license. We love the *Qur'ān* and the Prophet. But if we know the right time has not come, we can do nothing. The city has been taken over by rebels and every meter or so there is a landmine. It is estimated that there are something like five million landmines in Africa. So: we do not go out. We cannot say 'I have the *Qur'ān*, it is enough!' We simply do not go out. It is not the right season. We therefore have to judge the conditions, the ambience, and the environment. What if everything is all right but suddenly there is hail the size of a tennis ball? Unless we have an armored car, this car is going to be pierced.

It is helpful to bear in mind that the times we are living in now are like the first few years in Makkah, surrounded by denials and by enemies. You and I have the advantage of inheriting a great Islamic culture at a time when Europe and the rest of the world was in darkness. But we cannot simply rely on a heritage that has not been appropriately revived or continued. It does not mean we are also going to bow out and simply blame everybody else and be apologetic. The question is: are we are able to live with those values in spite of all these difficulties? If the answer is yes, then we are on the right path and there will be others who want to be with us.

There are two to three hundred odd *ayat* which come under approximately fourteen different categories. If we want to know the self and its model from the *Qur'ān*, we need to look at all the āyā*t* under *nafs, insān, nās, rūh, 'aql, qarin, qalb* and *fu'ād*. All of them are connected. They all tie up to make up a picture of the human self. For example, the verses on death describe who dies and what dies. The verses on *hayāt* describe the source of life. Thus we get a full picture.

The picture is very simple: everyone is made of a *rūh*, which is eternal and divine, and which has within it the patterns of perfections; but then its shadow and its echo is this individual human being – the you, I, he and she. Each one appears to be different, having come from different parents, at different times, yet we are all the same in terms of what we desire. What do we desire? We desire perfect contentment. That is why Allah addresses: '*yā ayyatuha'n-nafsi 'l-mutma'inna irja'ī ilā rabbiki radhiyatan mardiyah,*' 'O soul that is content, return to your Lord well-pleased (with Him), well-pleasing (to Him)' [89:27-28].

Allah says: 'We will soon show them Our signs in the Universe and in their own souls, until it will become quite clear to them that it is the truth. Is it not sufficient as regards your Lord that He is a witness over all things?' – *fi'l-āfāq, wa fi anfusihim'* [41:53]. Wherever you look is a message of Allah. *Lā ilāha illa'llah.* Allah is saying, 'I am the Creator. I am the Container. I am the Sustainer. And to me everything returns and by me everything has come.'

Our heritage is based on total and utter realization of *tawhīd.* From the one light have come infinite colors, rainbows and manifestations sustained by the same light. We are living in an age where scientists are beginning to discover the true meaning of oneness. If you and I do not relive our heritage, gain it, and acquire it by our desires, prayers and hopes, then we will miss it. And as Allah says: *'Allah will bring a people who love Him, and whom He loves.'* The entire thing will bypass us.

There is always both good news and warning. Allah tells the

glorious Prophet to first witness the truth. Witness the situation we are living in. Then give them the good news that you have come by Allah, by Allah's perfection you are carrying on, and to Allah's perfection you return. In the meantime, '*ya ayyūha 'l-insāna innaka kādihun ilā rabbika kadhā fa-mūlāqih*' – 'O man! Surely you must strive (to attain) to your Lord, a toiling hard striving until you meet Him' [84:6]. You are struggling towards what? Towards perfection. Everybody wants the ultimate in everything, like wealth. Absolute wealth belongs to Allah. Everybody wants on-going life – He is the ever-living and we all know our life is short. Everybody loves Him who is the most generous and Allah is beyond generosity – He is the only giver while we are all takers.

We have the heritage. We have the pattern. We have the map. We have the knowledge, but if we do not live it, it is like somebody going to a restaurant and arguing about the menu – this *madhhab*, that *madhhab*, this practice, that practice, and so forth – and they are not taking the vitamins! They are not taking the nourishment. They are only arguing and discussing until they leave this world when it is too late. This is the situation we find ourselves in.

But equally, this gives us an opportunity. Whenever there is a disaster or a difficulty it is also an opportunity, and even more so. That is the reason for the wonderful saying, '*In the country of the blind the one-eyed man is king.*' If we take a small look we will see ourselves excelling in every way. Allah's *rahmah* is great. At times of difficulties such as we are witnessing now, the *rahmah* and the forgiveness of Allah is greater. The Prophet tells his companions, '*If I tell you ten things and you forget one, you are in trouble, but a time will come that if people do only one out of the ten, Allah's forgiveness and mercy will be on them.*'

Every age has its counterbalance. If you were born in a community, in a small society where they were all pious and God-fearing, reciting and living the *Qur'ān* day and night, a small mistake showed up as a big sin. But at the time we are living in a little goodness will make us, in every way, excel. So we should see it is an opportunity.

So I thank Allah for the opportunity we have here for us to delve deeply into the teachings of the *Qur'ān*, into the teachings of the Prophet and to remind ourselves of the difficulty of the times and the responsibility upon us, each individually as well as families and brothers in the *dīn*.

I pray to Allah to enable us to share these teachings with others and to be a conduit for Allah's Mercy.

The entire foundation of knowledge is in the Qur'ān.

6: LIGHT AND DARKNESS IN MAN

All of creation is based on dualities & balanced opposites. The perception of darkness is due to the presence of light. The seeker of truth needs to focus more on light until darkness & illusions are banished.

Life is based on accepting what we desire and rejecting what we do not, attracting what we like and repelling what we do not. Everything we do and think of in this life goes in one of two directions: either we want it close to us or away from us. It is the same thing with ignorance – we want it to be far from us, which means we want knowledge to be near us. We want light close to us; we do not want shadows. We want to have certainty; we do not want to have uncertainty. The key and the door to this path is self-knowledge.

Allah has designed this human self in such a way that within it you will find every possibility that exists in the cosmos. Within it there is paradise and hell, good and bad, remembrance and forgetfulness, generosity and meanness. Now the key for us, as Muslims and *mu'mins*, is to read this map so that we do not constantly wander off the path as we are journeying towards the ultimate light.

The most important thing that we desire is the knowledge of this map so that we can follow it. Firstly, therefore, we have *'ilm al-yaqin*, the knowledge and certainty that this is the right map. This will lead us towards our safety, our inner joy, our *ma'rifah* – that is, to the knowledge that Allah is in charge so that we can relax. Secondly, we have *'ayn al-yaqin*: we have seen experientially that those who follow the map of true *tawakkul* (reliance) upon Allah, perfecting and doing their best in their worship and in character building and reforming themselves, are already successful. Thirdly, we have *haqq al-yaqīn*, when we are indisputably embedded in the truth of certainty. There is no longer a need for discourse. We know it is the only way that Allah has designed in His perfection for us to save ourselves from our own stupidity, our own arrogance and our own veils. Allah has given us so many verses in the *Qur'ān* in which He addresses *insān* (human beings) and *nās* (mankind); most of these are Makkan verses because they apply to everyone.

As the carpet of knowledge unfolded over the twenty-three years of the prophetic delivery of the message, we come across more verses incorporating '*ya ayyuha'l-mu'minu,*' or, '*ya ayyuha'lladhina āmanū*' (O you believer, or, O you who believe) because by that time the Prophet is addressing the Muslims. Thus the audience becomes more specific and the message is directed towards those who have already accepted the fact that there is One Creator by whose generosity and power all creation exists, by whose love and compassion we are now journeying to Him, by Him and unto Him. The specificity now increases. It is clear from the *dīn*, from the *Qur'ān* and the way of the Prophet that this *insān* has within him or her zones of darkness, ignorance, destructiveness, as well as zones of light, delight and pure perfection; Allah tells us in so many different verses that,

> ☼ 'And the soul and Him Who made it perfect [in balance].' [91:7]

Now here we come to the definition of the *nafs*. *Nafs is* also connected to breath – *nafas* is breathing. Here the word captures the idea of the fullness of the human soul or self. So Allah says what an amazing *nafs*: it contains within it, at the same time, the pattern of destructiveness and the pattern of acceptance and *taqwa* or recognition and acknowledgement of the laws and limits and who is in charge.

Allah tells us the story of how the angels were informed that he was going to create a representative on earth, i.e. mankind:

☼ 'And when your Lord said to the angels, I am going to place in the earth a *khalifah*, they said: What! Will You place in it such as shall make mischief in it and shed blood, while we celebrate Your praise and glorify You? He said: Surely I know what you do not know.' [2:30]

Allah had decided in His decree of '*Kun fa-yakun*' (Be and it is) that in creating a *khalifah* (or representative), He would be creating a creature that contains within it the entire patterns and designs of all other existence.

Angels are created according to numerous specific patterns; the *Qur'ān* describes some of them as having more wings, meaning more powers, or more propulsion. Angels are like electromagnetic pulses which activate other holographic entities in existence. So He says to them: 'You are specific and on clear channels, but this entity is my representative. When people do not see me, they can see my representatives – the closest to my qualities, which are the prophetic qualities.' Then the angels then object: '*Will You place in it [the earth] such as shall make mischief in it and shed blood...*' [2:30]. Meaning: 'Are you going to put on earth an entity that is going to slaughter and create havoc?' They had already foreseen all the despots as if they had already had a glimpse of all the so-called great 'democratic' leaders to come, in actual fact despots.

The angels continued their objection by saying: '*... while we celebrate Your praise and glorify You?*' meaning they could never deviate from the patterns that they were set on. Yet, this entity called man could deviate. Allah's answer was, '*...Surely I know what you do not know*' [2:30]. The implication here is that in the *insān*, in the *khalifah*, there is a zone called the *rūh* that knows and obeys the

Creator. Allah uses the word self in the *Qur'ān* to imply the *rūh* in the sense that He called all the *anfus* (pl. of *nafs*) and exposed them to the lower yet at the same time they acknowledge that Allah is their Lord – *'alastū bi rabbikum'* (Am I not your Lord?).

The *Qur'ān* uses the word *anfus* interchangeably with *arwah* (pl. of *rūh*). There is one pattern for the *rūh*: it has captured the divine qualities so the *rūh* knows the meaning of absolute generosity, the perfect life, foreverness, and *as-Sabūr* (the Ever Patient.).

The entire business of this life is based on time and space. We are prisoners of time and space, but within us lies the soul (*rūh*) that is from before time and space. It is for that reason the lower *nafs* has no *sabr*, no patience. It captures its energy from the *rūh* and the *rūh* is from before time and space, i.e. timeless and unlimited, so that is why the *nafs* is in a hurry, like a child. A baby or a child still remembers the *'Kun fa-yakun,'* so he screams: 'I want it now!' But as we grow accustomed to this prison of time and space, somebody who has reached ninety years old will say, 'Never mind a few years.' The young fellow, however, says 'I want to marry now,' but the grandmother says: 'No, wait five years,' because for her years are not important. She is getting close to returning to a zone where there is no time and space.

Another quality of the human being (*insān*) is also *nasiyan*, from the root meaning to forget. We forget that we came from the eternal garden into this world of change so that we get 'cooked' properly in order to return. A cake is not fully baked until it has been subjected to the torment of change and insecurity; we too so that we return to the one and only line of security of Allah, which is in the *rūh*. Our inside is made up of a *rūh* and a lower self – *'wa nafsin wamā sawwāhā'* (and the soul and Him who made it perfect [in balance]) – the *nafs* contains within it an element that knows what *taqwa* is, and what eternal bliss is, and another element which is tricky and *shaytānic*.

Then Allah says in the same chapter (*surah*): '*O Adam, dwell, you and your wife, in the garden, and eat from it abundantly wherever you wish...*' [2:35]. *Uskun* is from the root verb of *sakana*, to be quiet, to be content. *Sukūn* is silence, and therefore the circular symbol denoting silencing of a vowel in the Arabic script. *Maskan* is a house and a home is where passions are cooled, where you can rest, where you can unify the *nafs* and the *rūh*. The command to dwell with your partner means that the design of the human being can only be completed when duality is complemented by its opposite – because everything in this world is either one of two. It is either good or bad, man or woman, up or down, night or day, correct or incorrect, and they interchange. What is good for you now may not be good for you at another time. What is good for you in the month of *Ramadān* is not to think of food, but what is good for you on normal days is to remember food at lunch time so that you get your apple. We were created and designed for the eternal garden which was created for us.

Then Allah warns Adam that he has no needs in the garden, that he can simply takes what he wants, '*...and do not approach this tree, lest you be among the unjust*' [2:35] – the implication being that there is a 'zone' of consciousness of duality, of *shaytān* and *rahmān* and of good and bad. The word for 'tree', *shajarah*, is from the root verb of *shajara, yashjuru*, to quarrel. *Shijār* means quarrel, dispute or argument; it is as though the tree as it pushes itself up quarrels with the earth. It shakes it. If you speed up film, you will find it agitates the soil until it comes up. Adam, our glorious father, did not know what disruption, destruction and lies were. He did not know *shaytān*.

Allah in His mercy allowed *shaytān* to afflict us so that we turn to the *Rahmān* according to the program already fixed within us, which makes us want goodness, happiness and other qualities of the garden. So the work is already done in a perfect way. Before the rise of *shaytān*, Adam was in the eternal garden without knowing what hell was. With the completion of creation, every possibility was generated in it – not only good but also bad, which is easier for us to turn away from. Therefore we need *'ibādah,* worship and obedience, for our own sake.

Young people will accept ethics and morality once they know it is for their own sake. You can never impose the *dīn* on anyone. That is why it says: *'wa la ikraha fi'd-din'* (There is no compulsion in the *dīn*) [2:256]. We cannot force it, but once we know that by being correct and by not lying we will improve our own wellbeing, we will do it. Once we know that the less we are concerned about our physical, lower entity or sensuality, the more our minds and hearts are going to lead us into realms of joy, and then we will do it. But simply to force someone to do it, without the parents having done it, without having already applied it, is false.

So many of us are in a mess because we are not being transformed by our *dīn*; we are only stifling others with information and not following it ourselves. That is why if a community is not led from its own people as imams in the mosque we have to import some other less adequate preachers. We pride ourselves that our *dīn* has no intermediaries and yet as a result we have worse intermediaries than the others. We need to take the pulse of the patient constantly and understand what the sickness is so that the remedy will help; however, because we want to have an immediate remedy for everybody, the result is that we end up being accused of terrorism. We have to treat the case according to how it is created. If we do not know what the sickness is and what the priority of healing is, we will clumsily do no good to anyone.

The first people who need to live, enjoy and be illumined by their *dīn* are ourselves, and if we don't do it by ourselves it will remain a remote idea or some sort of a nostalgia, punctuated by outbursts of accusing others. It may make us feel better for a moment, but it is not going to give us sustained health. If something is good, we want it to be sustainable, not short-lived. We need on-going health, quality of heart, on-going elevation, brotherhood and love. It is no use people meeting each other and trusting each other for one minute because their pockets are full of money but the next minute accusing each other. Quick shallow friendship leads to quick enmity. We want slow, mature love. Let the friendship take a long time. It has taken us several years to establish a circle of people here who trust each other; if we cannot trust ourselves, how can we trust someone else, or trust Allah? Also, how can we trust ourselves if we cannot have some mirrors in other people whom we trust unconditionally for Allah's sake? That is why you find people get enthusiastic when there is a mosque to be built or a charity to be supported, but soon after that when it comes to the 'software' they start disappearing. Software requires total accountability to Allah and to those who know better than we do.

Be in constant awareness that Allah sees you, knows you, and is recording everything that is in you. Nothing exists for which He did not create its pair – its *zawj*. There is night and day. If there is cold, there is heat. If there is heat, then there is cold. If there is good, there is bad, with the two fluctuating constantly. Life in this existence is based on duality but the light behind all of these opposites is one. If we do not have access to that One Light, we will remain confused by the shadow and the *nafs*. The *nafs* is the shadow of the *rūh*. It is like a marriage: If there is mutual collaboration and love between the two, then they are one person. If not, one aspect says we should do this, another aspect says do something else; our child comes and blackmails us while the mother screams and the doctor is called, but we do not know who we are. If our direction (*qiblah*) is one – that is, to give ourselves and those who are close to us an opportunity to have a tranquil, wholesome heart, being ready to leave this world and to face any problem in this world – then the whole world will be under our feet. Thus the *dunya* becomes *ard* (earth). Allah warns us of the *dunya*, that which the lower self is attracted to – a bigger house or more cars. It is only going to give you more trouble – more thieves, more problems, more taxes to pay, more hassles and so forth. That is why the month of *Ramadān* is all about: 'less is more.'

Soon after that month, our inner aspect is more prepared to receive the ultimate truth that is beyond limitation. This world of limitation is only a sample of the world which is in us, which is limitless.

☼   'O you who believe! answer (the call of) Allah and His Messenger when he calls you to that which gives you life; and know that Allah intervenes between man and his heart, and that to Him you shall be gathered....' [8:24].

The believer is addressed: belief, *iman*, is connected to *amn*, which is contentment and security. So the implication is that those who are enjoying the comfort and ease of faith and trust should answer the call that beams within your own heart. We are called to that which is going to give us life, meaning life without end. We will continue after leaving this body, but in a different very simple fashion. There will be a *rūḥ* that is the same for all of us in a lamp with a glass over it, which is the *nafs*. If that lamp is clean, then we are clear. If that lamp is tarnished with all our desires, anxieties and *shaytāniyyah* (devilish antics) then the original light, the *rūḥ*, is covered by the darkness of the *nafs*. When we leave this body, it is the *rūḥ* and the *nafs* combined. If the *nafs* has been refined, groomed, put in its place, then it is healthy and we have no problems. When we know we have no problems, then we have no fear of death. That is how the early Muslims took the world because they had no fear of death. They were not suicidal. They were most respectful of the ultimate gift of Allah, which is life. But they knew real life is forever and that this life here is a temporary one, a prelude to the next.

Allah then reminds us: *'O Soul that art at rest...'* [89:27] – the *nafs* that has become certain that it has no power of its own but only from the *rūḥ* – *'...Now return to your Lord'* [89:28], because your Lord is ever there, His power, generosity and forgiveness is ever present. '...*Return to your Lord, well-pleased, well-pleasing (Him), so enter among My slaves and enter My Garden*' [89:28-30]. Now you are truly my connected, adored slave. You are now really doing your '*ibādah*; you are doing your worship in a total sense, not just by the tongue. '*And enter into My Garden*' – *Jannah* is from the root word *janna*, meaning to conceal or hide. The Arabic word has more than thirty or forty meanings, all of them relating to the unseen. For example, *janīn* is foetus – unseen by the human eye. *Majnūn*, meaning mad, because in that state the intellect is unseen or obscured. *Jannah* means a land in which you cannot see the earth, so richly covered is it with trees, flowers and foliage.

Allah describes the Garden's width as more than the heavens and the earth combined. Some of the ignorant people at the time asked if this was its width, then what might be its length? They started being rational! The answer was posed as a question: '*Where is night when day comes?*' *Jannah* is in you. It depends which of the buttons you are pressing. Press the button of anger and disappointment and your blood pressure goes up – hell. Press the button of, 'Allah knows best. Let me see what He is telling me, what His message is' – harmony and peace. His message may be to leave this place, this town, keep quiet, abstain or take it.

Allah says to the Prophet: '*So you did not slay them, but it was Allah Who slew them, and you did not smite when you smote [the enemy], but it was Allah Who smote, and that He might confer upon the believers a good gift from Himself; surely Allah is Hearing, Knowing*' [8:17]. He was the agent of Allah. And Allah tells us to do our *wājibāt*, or our necessary, obligatory prayers and worship and more until such time we have come so close that we are the ear by which He makes us hear and the hand by which He acts. In this way we become Allah's instruments. If we are Allah's instrument, then there is no concern, no grief. If we have grief, know for sure that we have stepped away from that connective beam of light. If we are sad or sorry, know that it is the *nafs*, it is not the *rūh*.

It is very simple. We have all the technology to be enlightened. We have the inner technology of illumination and enlightenment, but we have to apply it. Not that we do not know it is in the *Qur'ān*, but why is it not in our hearts? We have left the *Qur'ān* in a nice velvet case so that nobody can reach it. Allah describes it as *mahjūra* (abandoned) – we have left it behind. If we leave the Prophet behind we will end up under such despotic leadership as the world has witnessed.

Allah is telling us who we are. It is not a question of blaming somebody else. We must listen carefully to the message. Do not just obliterate it by excuses, reasons or blaming others: *'We will show you the signs on the horizons and within yourselves so you know'* [41:53]. Within yourselves you know now this is your grief speaking. Stop it then. Shaytan's usefulness is so that we turn back to Him, so that even when you have made a mistake you always say *subhanallah, subhanallah, subhanallah* – 'Allah has made me make a mistake so that I only 'take', and I do not 'miss' the take.'

And then we are told: *'And certainly We have set forth to men in this* Qur'ān *parables of every sort that they may reflect and understand'* [39:27]. Conscious, thoughtful awareness (*'aql*) is in us. The origin of the word is 'to contain'. *'Iqqāl*, from the same root verb, is this cord which the Arabs put around their head to keep their headscarf in place or to hobble a camel's leg. Nobody will receive these wonderful gifts of insight except those who have knowledge. What knowledge is that? The knowledge of the lower and higher self.

We want Light close to us; we do not want to follow our shadows.

7: THE ROOT OF WAR

Divine Oneness permeates the universe of dualities &
differentiations. Animosity & enmity are vulgar expressions of
oppositions and the plurality of shadows. When twos are seen
as expressions of the one there will be true harmony & peace.

I would like to share with you the meaning, effect and foundation
of the cause of conflict and the roots of war. As human beings we
all experience in our lives many occasions of discord, inner conflict,
outer conflict, uncertainty, and confusion. We oscillate between what
we consider to be good and what we consider to be bad. In this
life we all experience these constant, changing, opposing and yet
complementary opposites. After all, what is good for us now may not
be good for us tomorrow.

What is appropriate at this particular moment, where we are
endeavoring to share this inner knowledge, which is to be still and
silent, may not be appropriate when we are crossing a busy street. So
our values change according to our overall circumstances because at
all times we want to balance outer change with inner change to bring
about equilibrium between the outer situation and our inner needs
or expectations.

As Muslims, we have received the revealed knowledge and have
been taught that the cause of Prophet Adam (a.s.) coming down to
the world was his *ghaflah* (his distraction from being in the garden).
He was in the Garden in the most perfect situation. There was
no need for anything. Whatever he needed for that possibility of

complementarity or to bring about the perfection for his happiness was all there. In this perfect happiness he did not know what unhappiness or discord was. His coming down to earth was to see and experience the opposite, to and attain Allah's *Rahmah* (mercy), and for ourselves – mankind – to be completed by Allah's favor upon Adam (a.s.).

If we were perpetually in a perfect situation then we would only be experiencing half of the possibilities of creation. The other half is discord, a situation that is not conducive for long lasting inner peace and contentment. On this earth we are constantly seeking contentment and happiness and yet we all know intellectually, experientially, philosophically, as well as spiritually that lasting happiness, in the sense of complete and utter consistent inner tranquility, joy and happiness will not be attainable in this world. Nonetheless we foolishly continue to search for it. That is where *shaytanic* disruption and the trickery of misconception enter our lives.

Like Adam, we still continue to look for happiness, for that sense of inner equanimity, of absolute, unconditional security and contentment in the wrong place and in the wrong way. In the Garden needs were not known, desires were not known, nor was agitation, heat or movement; it was the perfect bliss of non-worldliness. This world, however, is entirely based on heat and movement. The hotter it is, the more likely it is to move into another zone of another consciousness. It is the same with movement: by going faster or slower change is induced. If you want to enter into the next consciousness, go as fast as you can until you go beyond speed. You must go faster than the speed of light, which is approximately 300,000 kilometers per second or have no movement at all, which is what we are supposed to do in *sajdah* (the prostration of prayer). When in this position you are at the threshold of the next phase of consciousness.

Allah describes this condition to be that of the original memory:

'*We will make you recite so you shall not forget*' [87:6] – this means remember or recollect before memory, that is, what was already impregnated in your *rūh* (soul) before the creation of this zone of time and space, with its finite beginning and end.

Allah tells us in the *Qur'ān*: '*We said: Go down from it, all of you*' [2:38]. His command is that we, or more specifically our *rūh*, existed originally in that zone of perfection but that then we should descend into apparent imperfection in order to realize that perfection was already there and that there is perfection within this apparent imperfection.

Then the *ayah* (verse): '*O mankind, what has deceived you concerning your Lord, the Generous*' [82:6]. Allah is questioning us: Who are you? What makes you arrogant about your Ever-Generous, Ever-Present, and Boundless Lord? What is this *ghurūr* (deception)? *Gharar* is also a name of *Shaytan*. Then Allah tells us the whole story about the self:

> ☼ 'And the soul and Him Who made it perfect, Then He inspired it to understand what is right and wrong for it.' [91:7-8]

The self has been designed so that it has within it its *taqwa*, its complete and utter reliance, confidence and alliance with its Origin. The spirit or the soul within us knows its Origin; it knows that it belongs to the garden, to a divine precinct which is boundless and pure light. But because it has been embodied in this world and is contaminated or amalgamated with this world's substance, that *rūh* has to have a cover, because it is pure light and pure light has to manifest as a rainbow or spectrum of lights, or in this case, as an identity that is called the self (*nafs*). The self is like a cover of glass on this non-material, non-physical light, which is called *rūh*, which the *Qur'ān* describes as emanating from 'the command of your Lord', and also that the *anfus* (the selves), which is the *arwah* (souls) in this *ayah* have all been exposed to and accepted: 'Am I not your Lord (*Rabb*)?'

The *rūh* knows all the attributes of the *Rabb* – the Ever Glorious, Ever Merciful, the Ever Loving, Most Generous, Ever Present, Maker, Creator, Taker, Giver. All of the divine attributes are in the *rūh*, or to put it another way, all the patterns of these attributes are in the *rūh* and the *rūh* has acknowledged them. Now this self, that is you and I as individuals, is different from other selves as individuals, but the same in their capacity as *arwah*. We have this magnificent tradition, which is often not understood by the Muslims, which says 'The souls are like Allah's soldiers'. Those souls that know each other will find affinity with each other and those souls who do not know each other will find enmity with each other. What does this mean? Allah tells us in the *Qur'ān* that the souls are the same. He says, '*We created you from one soul.*'

There are several other verses that reiterate the same principle of oneness. It is one self, one soul, but yet we are different selves. What this means is that the soul in us, that *rūh* in us, has in it the same pattern. Potentially the *rūh* of every one of us – be it the *mu'min*, the *kāfir*, the knower, and he who does not know – has in it divine knowledge. It is the cover of the *rūh* that must be groomed and purified. That is why the *nafs*, the lower self and the egocentric part of us, needs to be put in its place and disciplined. This is why we say it is subject to correct *'ibādah* (worship), and correct *bāy'ah* (obedience).

The lower self must obey the higher. Otherwise, we have the chaos which we observe in the world today. The root of every disturbance, the root of discord is due to the self (the Ego), not the *rūh* (The Soul). In fact we know it is the light of the soul shining on the Self and revealing that now there is chaos. Access to Allah is through the *rūh*, not the self. That is why you see people supplicating for years and nothing happens because it is the *nafs* supplicating, not the *rūh*. The *nafs* must yield to the *rūh*; it must die into the *rūh*, it must acknowledge the *rūh*, it must dissolve into the *rūh*, and the *rūh* will know that this is not the time to ask for people's mercy.

Allah says in the *Qur'ān* in several *ayat*, especially two addressed directly to the Prophet, that even if we make *istighfār* (seeking forgiveness) for people, nothing will be forgiven. We cannot because it is not the right time. They have gone off. The train is on a run-away track. How can we stop it? It is already destined to crash. It has gone off the rails and the driver is drunk! Now if we go and stand on the side and make supplications that it should go back on the track, it will not succeed. The process is too far gone.

Everything has its correct sphere of law; these are physical, chemical, biological and subtler or subatomic laws. Everything is subject to its own applicable sphere of law, to Allah's decrees. Allah's decrees are not going to change simply because we have been doing our *salāt* on time. We have to do our *salāt* on time regardless. *Salāt* is for our lower self to be obedient to our higher self because at the time of the *salāt* it may be inconvenient for the lower self because we may be concluding a business deal, or quarrelling, or we may be upset for some other reason. It is very inconvenient. So breaking off for *salat* disciplines the lower self. When *salāt* is called, we must stop whatever we are doing and do our *salāt* so that the lower self, the *nafs* or the ego realizes that the master is within it. This master is the *rūh* and the *rūh* is from *'the command of your Lord.'*

In this way, we begin to re-orient ourselves to our Lord. Discord, war and all the apparent destructiveness are a result of us not seeing the source of constructiveness. It is the disobedience of the self as far as the soul is concerned. The average religious person generalizes, saying that it is because they have 'gone off the *dīn*.' This is true, but it needs elaboration for the young, intelligent and questioning person.

Ask yourself why is there such misery within the Muslim countries, amongst the Arabs and throughout the world? What is the root of all this animosity? If we consider it from the point of view of the individual, we will discover that every person wants to remove whatever he or she perceives as an obstacle to his or her everlasting happiness. Whenever we have enmity towards someone or the urge to kill them it is because we perceive that person as a barrier to our constant, perpetual or everlasting happiness – they are a 'threat'. It is exactly the same when a nation wants to destroy another nation – we call it war.

This raises the question of what the meaning and the definition of happiness is. Happiness is when we feel in every way, totally, utterly, physically, mentally and spiritually in harmony. Ultimately, happiness is to do with ourselves. It is we who mislead ourselves by believing that if a certain woman won't love us, run after us and pamper us, we will be unhappy. It is we ourselves who have created this unhappiness. It is the meaning we give. For other people, this woman may not mean anything; their happiness would be otherwise defined.

So it is our own inner universe that needs to be put right, not the outer universe – but we do not see this so we blame her and quarrel with her! The poor woman is Allah's instrument to show us that we are looking in the wrong direction for the right thing. You are seeking perpetual happiness but in the wrong place. The truth is that you have to laugh at yourself and be sorry for all the years that have gone by and then you can perform your *salāt* properly.

The root of discord is misguided expectations. Our original search for the Adamic condition of being in the Garden where we have no needs is correct. We are all driven to seek that state of continuous inner access to a steady and constant zone that reassures us that everything is alright even if we do not know why it is happening. If we just wait a minute we will come to know why. People quarrel because they are all looking at the same elephant, but they are blind and as one of them holds the trunk he says it is a rope, the other one holds the leg and says it is a pillar, and the third holds an ear and says it is like a flat sheet. They argue with each over these differences that are, in actuality, merely apparent but not real differences because it is one elephant.

It is the same with all of us human beings: we each, every one of us, want the certainty that there is a zone of constant inner security and joy. This is why Allah describes our glorious Prophet as 'a mercy to creation' so that we may know that the way we are pursuing our life is destructive. If we go to the Creator we will find what we need; if we expect anything from creation we will be disappointed. Go for the One and the rest will be alright, but go for the 'two' and nothing will be right. That is why human beings are programmed such that if someone comes to us and constantly asks for something, we resent it. So do not ask of creation, ask the Creator. Allah loves to be asked, but human beings do not. With us it is exactly the reverse. In fact, we like the person who gives us a gift every time we meet him. The Prophet says that human beings are 'abidu'l-hisāb, meaning that if you do goodness unto someone you will own them.

Ask the higher in you for what is true and you will always receive an answer; but it must be real, it must be true, it must be from your soul, not from your *nafs*. The soul has direct access to all the Divine Attributes while the *nafs* is playing in its shadow and is therefore always chasing something that can never be attained by it. The difference in this aspect is the difference between *dunya* (worldliness) and *ard* (earth). *Dunya* is that which you and I love to have because we are actually trying to mimic the *rūh*, and the *rūh* is the *'arsh* (Throne) of Allah. That is why we say our heart must be pure because it is the home of the *rūh*.

☼ 'Allah is the Light of the Heavens and the earth. The likeness of His light is as a niche within which is a lamp...' [24:35]

We realize that the human potential is that. Allah says in a divinely revealed tradition: *'My heavens and earth cannot contain Me, but the heart of he who trusts and believes in me (the mu'min) contains me,'* meaning our *rūh* contains all the attributes of Allah. Our Prophet says: *'Do not discuss Allah, discuss Allah's attributes'.* Discuss Allah's qualities, His Patience, His Subtlety (*lutf*), His closeness, His unconditional love for His entire creation and so on. These are all in our *rūh*. That is why if somebody reflects some of these attributes, such as when he is generous or patient, we love that person.

Likewise we often exaggerate those qualities because the *rūh* wants to show the highest in everyone. That is why when people talk about someone who is dead they exaggerate his good habits and ignore most of his miserable ones, quite rightly, because we want to honor the soul and not the *nafs*. So we ignore the *nafs*. We want to honor the soul. The soul is to be honored because it is *min amri rabbi* (from the command of my Lord). The *nafs* is the shadow of it and is to be dishonored. Dishonor the lower and the higher is already honored. This is the purpose of the journey. If we do not fulfill that purpose we will be confused and eventually become suicidal in every way. Some people may end up terrorizing others because they are not reconciled within themselves.

If you are not reconciled within yourself and add more and more agitation to the self it will burst. The root of animosity, enmity and war is none other than looking in the wrong direction for the right thing, looking for inner contentment and happiness but expecting to discover it in the self. The self cannot give it to you. The self will only confuse you and abuse you more. That is why *'ibādah* is vital because worship, done correctly, is transformative.

We Muslims have not been fully transformed because we are suffering from expectations, from information. Like every other culture, we have an information overload. The clash of cultures now between the so-called Muslims and non-Muslims is because the Western system has reduced this incredible human potential to nothing other than a mere economic entity. It is a system and a way of life that cannot last and that is why they have to invent wars. They had the Cold War with the communists and now it is against the Muslims. Muslims are failing constantly because they have not completely absorbed their Islam and are not living it. We are still living with the memories of the glorious 'golden' days, but for the last two to three hundred years we have been decaying. If we do not renew and revive our heritage and re-embrace our *dīn*, we will lose the opportunity. We have the genetic and the cultural inheritance, but we must uphold their value. We cannot simply inherit them. It is like someone who is a rascal and a criminal but talks about his great parents; he is in fact a disgrace to his parents.

Allah reminds us: 'O *self at rest! Return to your Lord, well-pleased, well-pleasing (Him)'* [89:27-28]. He is calling upon the soul that is in leadership now. As you know, the *nafs* has so many different facets – the *nafs al-ammarah* (commanding self) is the ego of a child saying, 'I want this immediately, give it to me!' It is when the poor wife who has to rush because her husband has called for his coffee again, and if she does not fetch it immediately he threatens her with violence or divorce. Once the child begins to grow it begins to understand that this behavior is not going to work. With age, changing hormones, maturing of the mind, discipline, education and parental guidance, the self becomes *nafs al-mulhamah* (inspired self), but before that it is *nafs al-lawwamah* (blameworthy self), blaming itself and apologizing – 'I am sorry mama, I didn't need to do all that.'

Fortunately as Muslims, we do not have guilt; we say it is heedlessness or *ghaflah*. We are human beings who have been distracted from the Garden so therefore we have to return to the Garden. The Christians have original sin and the guilt that comes with it. Coming from the same Abrahamic family, we all – Jews, Christians and Muslims – have the fall of Adam. They all mean

roughly the same thing but we have the clearer picture: the fall of
Adam is to prepare for his rise, the fall of the soul into the encasement
of the self is for it to realize that this is only a small temporary shield
designed to do a job until it is mature. Then we realize that the self
within us is always selfish and opposed to the high qualities of the
soul. Your *nafs* always has in it some higher qualities, but the *rūh* is
your command over the lower self. You can only return because you
have completed your job – return to your Lord who is always there.
Radiyah – you are now content. *Mardiyah* – you know everything is
content with you, you know your Lord is content with you.

If we do not complete that process we will remain stuck in the
current situation of global confrontation, which is entirely based on
denying our faults. Western civilization does not want to admit its
fault in reducing the human being to a little consuming animal with
an outer civilized face but vicious, violent, rampaging, non-ending
inner desire. All their industries abroad, all of their sports, games,
entertainment, and businesses, are based on endless, all-consuming
ambition.

It is Allah's message that you are not supposed to damage other
people's property no matter what! In the first seven or eight years
of his public life in Makkah, the Prophet never accused anybody
of anything. We must imagine in those years he was surrounded by
people full of denial. Many Muslims today are also in denial. They
deny their own faults. We deny our inadequacy in not having lived
up to our *dīn*.

So there is denial versus denial and there is war. Denial will only
bring about the projection of our faults and inadequacies onto the
'other '; it is as simple as that. That is why confrontation never ceases.
We follow our egos. As long as we keep remembering the *ākhirah*
(the Hereafter), however, that this life is temporary, that we are going
back to the abode of the Garden, and this is only a preparation for
that, then inner knowledge that all is well and as it should be will

take root within us. Then we become light upon light continuously, and the more we see shadows the more it reinforces the light within us. If there are enough people like us there will be a community; the influence will be real, not by enforcing it. By Allah's decree it will become effulgent.

Everyone in this world loves to be in a situation where they can stay happy and easily deal with unhappiness, outer difficulties, discord, and change. Yet it is in the nature of this world to change, as while we are at all times looking for happiness that never changes, so we are looking for the right thing but in the outer sense. We need to look for it in the inner sense. Allah shows us that the outer is flimsy and short-lived, but not to be denied. But we are warned not to become like so many other communities whose teachings were distorted, as was the case with early Hinduism, with the assertion that this outer does not exist. Of course it exists, but its existence is temporary and contingent in order to lead us to that which is permanent. If we deny the temporariness and the difficulty, we will be denied everlasting ease in our hearts. The heart has to always be left intact. Once we have taken the world into our hearts, the light of the soul, which is in the heart, cannot shine into us, for it will have become tarnished.

This is why we need to have proper discipline, clear minds, pure hearts, and accountability to others. We need to have a community of others that reflect back to us; otherwise we may go astray. When the soul is not obeyed, when the soul is not effulgent, when the soul is not in leadership, then the *nafs* can go on the rampage and it will justify everything. This is Allah's creation; once we see the map we will laugh at the self, we will laugh at the ego and be disgusted with it. And then we will be honored and in every way illumined and in joyful gratitude to the everlasting soul which will leave our body when the time is right, covered by the shell of the *nafs*. If the *nafs* has been purified and is polished to nothing other than a clear glass, then it is *rūhun wa rayhān*. There is no question; the angels questioning us will be redundant. If not, then we go through another process which we do not know exactly how– it is further refining and burning for purification. That is Allah's domain: we do not know what happens in the grave, how much turmoil and disturbance there will be. So let us live the disturbance now and be done with it so as to reach a point of inner tranquility.

Hope is that which is accompanied by action, otherwise it is merely wishful thinking.

8: THE DOORWAY TO FORGIVENESS

To forgive is to cover what was wrong or unjust with what is good and generous. Allah radiates these qualities.

To understand the meaning of *istighfār* (forgiveness, covering up faults), there are certain other things we need to understand first. In life and in existence, the most important factor of being in balance and equilibrium is to see things as they are so that we do not become confused. Our Prophet often used to repeat the supplication of wishing to see things as they are. The poison of a snake can also be a remedy; it is not evil or bad in and of itself. When you sometimes consider yourself to be in constriction and difficulty it may be the best thing for you. Allah says that something that you and I may consider to be hard, difficult and undesirable may be the best thing for us: *'...and it may be that you dislike a thing while it is good for you, and it may be that you love a thing while it is evil for you, and Allah knows, while you do not know.'* [2:216] We must see things as they are, not as we think, imagine or wish it to be. This is Allah's way.

Our business as Muslims and *mu'mins* is to read the road map of reality and understand it. Read Allah's existential atlas. Everything has its cause and effect. If you turn this way, this is what happens and if you turn that way that is what happens. If we do not follow this we will destroy our bodies, our minds and our hearts (the most important aspect). Allah's design is such that the human beings, the sons of Adam, are essentially and potentially His *khalifahs* (representatives or stewards) on this earth.

The *khalifah* has a responsibility towards his own self and towards creation to know that the creator, Allah, sees it all, knows it all, witnesses it all and is recording it within us as well. The human being is reflecting the entire cosmology. If we reflect properly, we realize that whatever we experience outside has its essence, its origin or its pattern inside. Otherwise, we would not be able to 'experience' it. It is a great affair, a great gift and a great creation that Allah has endowed us with. It is for this reason that we cannot but end up in gratitude.

Reading the map is essential. The first thing in that reading is the nature of *insan*, of the human being. Allah repeatedly tells us in the *Qur'ān* that our nature is *da'īfa* (weak), *jahūla* (ignorant), and all of the other lower attributes. Essentially we are mean, impatient, forgetful and weak. Why did Allah in his great wisdom create human beings with these basic lower tendencies? This is where the path of *Islām*, *Īmān* and *Ihsān* begins. It is by first realizing that we have nothing of our own, that basically we have come into this world with no possessions or power of our own and that we will also leave in the same way. In the meantime, what have we acquired and what have we learnt? Are we wiser? Are we enlightened? Are we content inwardly? Are our hearts as Allah desires or wishes them to be: *qalbun salīm* (content heart), or *qalbun sakīn* (tranquil heart)? We are in this intermediate *barzakh*, an intermediate stage between two realms, that is, we have come from the unknown of the womb and we leave for the unknown of the tomb.

The purpose of the message and the messenger, the desire of Allah and His expectation of us, is for us to wake up to the presence, uniqueness, ongoingness and everlastingness of Allah. That is the entire business. When Allah says: *'I did not create Jinn and mankind except to worship me'* [51:56]. He means that we should know Him, adore Him and have nothing other than passionate *'ishq* (undivided love) for Him, so that the *'ishq* of *dunya* and other things will not distract us from our real purpose.

Look at His perfect design. He has made us love beauty or beautiful things. He has made us love things that last, like friendships, because He is the Everlasting. They are all reflections of His attributes. That is why we are reminded in numerous places in the *Qur'ān* to recognize and admit our weakness, and then remember Allah's power which pervades everything. Through our illness we call upon His *Shifā'* – for He is *al-Shāfī* (the Healer). Through our discontent and insufficiency, we call upon *As-Samad* (the Eternally Self-Subsistent*)*. Through our confusion of *tafriqa* (separation) and of all the differences, we call upon his *Uhudiyya,* or *Wahadiyyah,* or *Ahadiyya (*Oneness/Unity). It is by realizing the lower nature of the *insān* that we can and will be guided and pointed towards the higher qualities of the Creator of *insān.*

The design is very simple and He has already perfected the entire thing. What you and I have to do now is to follow. We have in our great heritage of Islam, tremendous emphasis on following, being obedient, obeying and accepting. How can anybody accept anything unless they know it is good for him or her? What is good for us? The ultimate reference point of good or bad is that which is going to last. We want lasting health. We want lasting, durable relationships. We want lasting reference points. There is no point in having five minutes of pleasure and paying the price for five years.

We all want *sa'ādah* or happiness. Allah says in a divinely revealed *hadīth: 'I created you for eternal happiness (sa'ādah abadiyyah).'* What we are looking for is the eternal garden. In this world we do our best to avoid the fire and experience the garden. Ultimately, those who move higher and higher in *'irfān* (gnosis) and inner knowledge discover that the garden is within themselves. The entire cosmos is within us and the reason we are not experiencing that unity is that the gross or outer prevails over the subtle or inner. If you have a pain in your toe, you cannot have a clear mind. If you have a disturbed mind, you cannot have a pure heart. The disturbed mind takes over. It makes you suspicious of everybody and judgmental of everybody else, except your own stupidity.

The path of Allah, the design of Allah, is that you and I have to care for every aspect in a hierarchical order. We first have to pursue the command to cleanse our outer, our clothes, skin, food, our intake – *thiyabaka fatahhir* ('and purify your garments'); then comes our mind and then our heart. Now the secret of the heart is that it is the house and the abode of the *rūh* and the *rūh* is *min amri rabbi* (by the command of my lord). It has in it all the heavenly and all of the divine frequencies. It is unending light upon light. If the heart is clear and cleansed, then the *rūh* will emit its light fully and will energize the self so that the self recognizes its lower nature – *ammarah* or *lawwāmah*. So we say: 'I know my Self. It contains all the animal tendencies.'

Then you have the witnesser in you, the *shāhid*. *Shāhid* is a witnesser. In describing the *yawm al-qiyāmah* (Day of Reckoning or Resurrection), Allah says that every self comes witnessing itself and driving itself forth – *sā'iqun wa-shāhid* – 'And every soul shall come, with it a driver and a witness' [50:21]. *Sā'iq* is the driving force and impelling power. We have no power of our own except what Allah has given us, through the *rūh*. The more you are aware, the more the witnesser in you becomes aware. That is why a person who is pious, who is *muttaqi*, will not transgress by punishing others, shouting or being angry. Immediately the *shāhid* within says: 'Look. It's enough. You have made you point and it is now enough.' So, we have a witnesser in us which is a result of reflectiveness and introspection. We become present.

The heart has these different facets that transmit to the self, like lights or like mirrors. As well as the witnesser, there is also the *raqīb* (monitor). These facets are all to be found in the *Qur'ān*. Not only is Allah referred to as the *raqīb* but also the Prophet. We have in us another part of ourselves that monitors us. This tells us when to stop, go away or leave. Then it is not just a witnesser, but an intervening higher self.

After understanding this background, we come now come back to *istighfar*. *Istighfar* is part of *'ibadah* or worship. *'Ibadah* is recognizing the low while appealing to the high, recognizing my weakness and appealing to Allah's strength and power to cover it. Like most of these terms, we have to refer to the original Arabic. The word *ghafara* in Arabic means to cover, and from has come to mean forgive. *Ghufra* is what you cover your head with. The word in Arabic for head cover, as well as a helmet, is *maghfir* or *mughfir*, a thick protective head covering. When someone died it is said of him *maghfuranlahu*, meaning that though death his faults have now been covered and we can no longer see them. Then *ghafir* means watchman, i.e. he who will cover you from the onslaught of evil at night. So the Arabic word is not simply to 'forgive'. It means to overcome weakness and inadequacy. So when you recognize your hastiness and you say *astaghfirullah* it means that we ask Allah's infinite patience or Allah's timelessness – *huwa 's-Sabur* – to cover my inadequacy and hurriedness. It is for that reason, the Prophet says: 'The best of *du 'a* is *istighfar*.' It is the foundation to cover our normal, lower human tendencies.

It is Allah's perfect design that alongside us having lower tendencies – forgetfulness, nastiness, suspicions – it is also His higher qualities that we adore and love and so we desire to cover our lower tendencies. So in the sense of programming the work is already done. All we need to do is to follow it. The best of *istighfar* – the best of asking Allah to cover us, forgive us or to pardon us – is that we never repeat and regret what we have done. *'Your Lord knows best what is in your hearts; if you are good, then He is surely Forgiving to those who turn (to Him) frequently'* [17:25] A child goes to the electric socket once or twice and he or she gets a shock until eventually he or she learns that this causes trouble and injury. Nobody wants to be shocked. The same thing with human beings: if we know the trouble that comes to us from greed, we will stop being greedy. We have to suffer and then we take Allah's offer. This is already done.

Allah also says in the *Qur'ān*: *'And ask forgiveness of Allah; surely Allah is Forgiving, Merciful'* [4:106]. Turning to Allah accompanies sincere asking of forgiveness. *Atūbū* means 'I repent' or turn in repentance, that is, to return. Another verse tells us that: Allah is quick to account: *'That Allah may requite each soul (according to) what it has earned; surely Allah is swift in reckoning'* [14:51]. Whatever you do is in you and it is going to be accounted for. Escape is impossible. Whatever we think or do, great or small, is going to be registered in us. We are the carriers of our past actions. Then Allah says that He is All Forgiving and has only Mercy.

We are endowed with other attributes of shame and of guilt. Shame is a dynamic feeling that arises when are doing something which we know that we could have done better. Feeling ashamed means we know Allah's higher qualities and yet we are practicing our lower qualities. Guilt comes after the event. Guilt is that we did something and we know we could have done better. The bigger the gap between what we did and what we could have done better is the extent of our guilt.

All of these come under the umbrella of Allah's cover. Allah's protection and care is forever covering us. It is only we who go to the past and resurrect the dead. That is why the true *mu'min* regrets at the time, asks Allah's forgiveness and moves on. We don't constantly go and visit the scene of the crime. Expect the best of Allah and remember that one of His qualities as it is described in the *Qur'ān* is *al-'Afuw*. It is from the word *'afā*. It means effacing, obliterating, or wiping out, and hence, to pardon. From the same word *'afuw* comes *'āfiyah*, meaning wellbeing. The past doesn't exist anymore because time, in reality, doesn't exist. It is only as part of His 'catchment', so that we are in time and space yearning for non-time and non-space. Amnesty in Arabic is also from the same word as to pardon. When somebody issues an amnesty to the public it is called *'āfuān*.

Though in reality the past does not exist, we are the product of it. In so far as we are the evidence it is relevant, but no more. The rest is mental sickness and the emotional stupidity of going back and forth in time – which robs us of presence. That is why one of the main conditions of a *salāt* that truly energizes us is *hudūr* (presence) of our hearts. That is why when we do *wudu* we stop connecting with the world and are now totally and utterly connected through our hearts and our *rūh* to our Creator – this helps us be present. All the ritual practices of Islam enhance our presence; they make us reflect and available totally. The only contact we have with Allah is now. Yesterday is of no use and we don't know if we will be here tomorrow or not. The only gift we have is the present moment. If the moment is fully and utterly treasured then we are at the gateway of eternity.

Allah reminds us that this business of *istighfār* is a personal one. We are all striving towards Allah, to know the incredible high qualities that we love and aspire to – His perfection. We are reminded that: *'Surely Allah does not cover the fault if you are associating anything with Him, and forgives what is besides that to whomsoever He pleases; and whoever associates anything with Allah, he devises indeed a great sin'* [4:48]. We recognize 'somebody' is doing it, but that person has no independent power. He is doing it because Allah allowed it to happen. The entire business is *tawhīd*. If we see the One, then we can deal with the two. If we only try to deal with the two, we miss both. The two and the one cannot cover us.

Then look at this incredible situation described in the *Qur'ān* where there are several *ayat*, principally two clear ones, when the Prophet is asked to help other people for *istighfār*: *'...Our Lord! surely we believe, therefore forgive us our faults and save us from the chastisement of the fire'* [3:16]. Allah says: *'...Allah will blot out out the falsehood and confirm the truth with His words; surely He is Cognizant of what is in the breasts'* [42:24].

And furthermore: 'It is alike to them whether you beg forgiveness for them or do not beg forgiveness for them; Allah will never forgive them; surely Allah does not guide the transgressing people' [6:36]. Surah Munafiqun is about the hypocrites: not serious. How can a person who is fooling around or being totally irresponsible receive that healing power of covering? It means that everyone is responsible for himself, or herself. We can only show them the way and remind them that Allah is ever forgiving. But we must ask for it ourselves and put our past behind us. We must have regret and remorse, otherwise the forgiveness doesn't happen. We cannot tell someone go ahead and commit every foolish act and I will ask Allah to forgive you.

There is another *ayah* which further illustrates this. The *munāfiqūn* (hypocrites) in Madinah were a big issue. Rich people were giving money and the poor people were giving what little they could. The *munāfiqūn*, especially the leader and Abdullah ibn 'Ubey and many others, fooled around so much that this verse was also revealed: *'Whether you ask forgiveness for them or do not ask forgiveness for them; even if you ask forgiveness for them seventy times, Allah will not forgive them; this is because they disbelieve in Allah and His Messenger, and Allah does not guide the transgressing people'* [9:80]. It doesn't mean that the Prophet will do that. The Prophet is Allah's reflection. The Prophet is *Insān al-kāmil*, he is the perfect man. He knows that. So it is not that if the Prophet asked Allah it would not be accepted, but Allah will only be asked by the Prophet when it is already done, when it is already in synch with the right pattern of Allah's creational map. It is like somebody driving recklessly down a mountainous road, losing control and goes crashing down a canyon; everything is smashed and he says: 'Now please, get me back.' It doesn't work like that. Everything has its ecology, and its own cosmology and its laws. The bumps and jolts along the road are warnings – 'Look out!

Reduce your speed.'

Istighfār means that we have personal responsibility. We have to regret our actions, want to change, realize our lower tendencies, and then ask Allah to cover it. Then it is *'ibadah*. Otherwise, like many other things which people ask of Allah, nothing happens because the courtesy is not there. It is like somebody trying to call on a cell phone: if the battery is not charged, if we haven't paid our subscription or if we don't know the number we are calling nothing will happen. We will fumble and mumble from now until eternity. We must know we are addressing Him who has designed the entire cosmos, known and unknown. It is He who knows what we are doing. It is He who hears what we are saying. If He already knows our state, then we are already in an intimate *munājāt* (dialogue), not just frivolously asking, 'O *Allah give me this, and make me president of that.'*

So the courtesy or the *adab* of *istighfar* is in realizing our mistake, not wanting to repeat it and pleading to Allah to cover our faults. Then it becomes important and the most critical foundation upon which we build our worship. As Muslims we all have access to this technology of transformation. The key is to apply it properly. We listen to a radio program or watch TV diligently but we don't read and apply and live our *Qur'ān* fully, or follow the way of our glorious Prophet. We turn it into a mixture of rituals, emotional goodwill and good feelings, or good intentions. But unless it is going to be transformative, not just informative, we will remain backward and in every way mixed up, confused, angry about the past, angry with parents and angry at circumstances. The key is to read the map and then apply it properly, know where we are and at which junction. What is it we need now? Do we need more subduing, more constriction, more silence, more *'ibadah*, more restriction, more fasting or more teaching? We need to become aware of what it is we need, so that we move on, until such time we truly know that Allah is with us. Never has your Lord ever left you alone. Then it is not a question anymore of saying 'I have faith.' We know that Allah knows that we don't know and that he knows what we need to know and that he will give it to us at the time we need to know. The business is done. These are the signs of arrival. Allah says: *'We are nearer to him than his jugular vein.'* [50:16]

We must ask ourselves what is the journey we are taking? He is already there. We have been deflected. We are looking elsewhere. Stop looking elsewhere. Be present. Do your *sajdah* properly. Disappear into His light and you will be overflowing with the joy of His being present in your heart. Allah says in a divinely revealed tradition: *'My heavens and the earth cannot contain me, but the heart of him who has total faith and trust contains me.'* We must take responsibility. We must have urgency. This moment may never return. The companions we have, our friends, the *jama'ah* we love or the place we have been learning from may not be there later. Other events may take over. So live the moment urgently and ask Allah's constant *ghufrān* and His constant generosity of *karam* and *jūd* to cover us.

> **The Prophet used to say:**
> **'O Allah! Let me see things as they are.'**

9: THE MEANING OF RITUALS IN ISLAM

All actions, intentions & outcomes are connected. In acts of worship too our rituals, their meaning & influence upon our lives are ever-connected. The outer package is as good as its inner content.

I acknowledge my gratitude to the Creator, Sustainer and He who guides His creation to the purpose for which He has created them. Allah has declared to us as Muslims and *Mu'mins* and that the purpose of this creation is to worship Him. The first basic principle before we can build any additional guidelines on them is that the foundation of existence is based on *Tawhīd.* This means that there is none other than He Who has created, is sustaining and controlling the seen and the unseen, the worlds that we know and the worlds that we do not know.

The human being (*ins*) and the unseen being (*jinn*), the past, present and the future, are all in His hands. Allah created out of mercy and compassion, so that we, His ultimate creation – the sons and daughters of Adam – yield and submit to His will. We will thereby become united with Him and not constantly move from one extreme anxiety to another, for example, fear about our provision, relationships or the material world (*dunya*). We all have to deal with this world and cannot escape relating, acting, earning, being concerned about our families, children, home, transport, and whatever else that is involved in living and existing.

All of us, rich and poor, mighty and weak, are caught in the need to act and have the right intention and take the right actions. Nobody can escape that as long as we are in this world. It is no different for me: I have a family and I am also a concerned father. The times we are living in where the poisons of this irreligious (*kufr*) system comes down to every household through media, games, drugs and other forms of abuse, and through the misrule of politicians makes us all collectively suffer. The collective *kufr* system is now everywhere.

We Muslims who love our way of life (*dīn*), who love the Creator, who are at all times humble, who love our Prophet Muhammad , who want to know what to do under these circumstances have an advantage, however. The time we are living in also gives us a tremendous advantage in that we have witnessed, experienced, learnt, read and received hundreds of years of history of good living by other Muslims. A lot of it was also hard living, not pampered and not in luxury. As we know Allah declares in the *Qur'ān* that when the time comes for people to vanish, or be recycled, the rulers amongst them live in such luxury and corruption that it leads to their destruction – and that their account is with Allah. We have an incredibly rich and very privileged tradition, but we must put it in the right perspective. It is no good simply longing for the perfect times as Prophet Muhammad – as the *Qur'ān* describes it: *'You were the best of people...'* [3:110]

We cannot sit back and just weep, but we need to do what we can in the time we are living in. These are very difficult times, in that we are often earning our keep in a *haram* (unlawful) way, without maybe realizing it. The banking system is unjust (*harām*). The way we are handling money and usury dominates us. There is very little blessing (*barakah*) in what we do. Some people end up earning much more but they feel less and less satisfied. Much of it is spent on medicine, accidents or insurance and all the other things that are superfluous and irrelevant.

We Muslims have a great advantage if we live our Islam; meaning that, first and foremost, as grownups we realize that though we are limited beings, we are reflectors of the truth (*haqq*). Allah has the power (*qudrah*), intention and will. He is *as-Samī', al-Basīr* – He hears and sees – and so do we, but our hearing and seeing is limited. Our ability is limited whereas Allah's *qudrah* is infinite. It is beyond our capacity to comprehend. That is why we declare all the time, 'Allah is the greatest *(Allahu Akbar)'*. Allah is greater than we can imagine, because He has created our imagination. How can the created have access to, limit and delineate and define the source?

This is *Islam* (to surrender*). It is submission to our inadequacy. It is submission to the way Allah has created us. He says in the *Qur'ān* '*Allah desires that He should make light your burdens, and man is created weak.'* [4:28]. That is why our father Adam succumbed to the voice of the devil (*Shaytan*). Adam was innocent. He had never heard a lie in the Garden, so when he heard *Shaytan* he thought it was telling him the truth – 'Go for this tree, the tree of eternity.' He was already in the garden of eternity! Allah has created and allowed *Shaytan* and its evil whispers (*wiswas*), so that by choice we submit to the All-Merciful (*al-Rahman*). We have no choice in that all of us have this submission in our innate nature (*fitrah*).

That is why it is so important to have a grasp of some of these Arabic *Qur'ānic* terms used. If there is going to be a true revival, as I know there is already in the *nation* (*ummah*) of Muhammad, it is going to be based on returning to the original way of Muhammad, which includes also using the Arabic terms. It does not mean that we have to learn all the different dialects of the Arabic languages. It means we have to learn and understand the *Qur'ānic* terminology. Our way of life is the *dīn* of Allah. Allah says: '*Surely the (true) religion with Allah is Islam'* [3:19].

What is Allah's will? Allah's will is for us to be truthful. Truthful to what? To our weakness, to our pleading to Allah, to our trust that Allah will save us, to our trust that the next life will be better, to our trust that tyranny, abusiveness and lies will not last. This trust is submission to these truths. We have to <u>live</u> our Islam. And our Islam is founded on *taqwa*. This word cannot be translated into English easily. The best definition of *taqwa* I have found is constant cautiousness. Allah says:

> ☼ 'And they planned and Allah (also) planned, and Allah is the best of planners'. [3:54]

Allah's ways will prevail. And what are Allah's ways? What does He want of us? He wants us to adore Him, worship Him and submit to Him. That is the foundation of Islam.

Islam is not just a few rituals. Islam is transformation – our knowing that Allah is there, He sees, hears, guides. He is the Beneficent (*ar-Rahman*), the Most Merciful (*ar-Rahīm*), He is the ever-Providing (*ar-Razzāq*), the Bestower (*al-Wahhāb*), the Coverer of all Faults (*al-Ghaffar*), the all-Forgiving (*al-Ghafur*).

Our knowing it is different from simply saying it. There's a big difference between professing and living our Islam, which means faith and trust (*īmān*). We are illumined by our faith. It is not just some idea we have. Faith starts as an idea that there must be a purpose to this life, but when it becomes belief, we know, we are certain that when we have come to an end not knowing where to turn, Allah will send us a signal. This is the advantage of the believer (*mu'min*). *Imān* comes from from *amn*, the Arabic root is to be content in the knowledge that we are safe, that Allah is in charge. He is the Lord (*Rabb*) and we are the slave and servant (*'abd*), but the foundation of it is submission to our limitations, submission that this life is short, submission that we can never find perfection here, submission to the truth that this life is not just for comfort and ease. Occasionally, however, we will get comfort and ease when we rest, when we sleep, when we are with the true lovers of Allah, our brothers in the way of Allah and the sisters between themselves and with the relationship between husband and wife, which are complementary.

This life is a practice for us to return to the eternal Garden. For that reason we all love gardens, but ultimately the garden is not just a place: it is a state, a condition in our heart. There are so many outer gardens that people enter and only quarrel there. They end up more miserable than before. So the *mu'min* believes that Allah who knows all will give him what he needs to know. The *mu'min* knows he is weak. We have little knowledge but Allah is the all-Knowing (*al-'Alim*), so what we need will be given to us at the appropriate time. For that we have to be correct and sincere (*ikhlās*). Without sincerity who are we trying to fool? That full and total sincerity will lead us to Allah's promise in the *Qur'ān*, that it is He: '...Who answers the distressed one when he calls upon Him and removes the evil, and He will make you successors in the earth. Is there a god with Allah? Little is it that you mind!' [27:62].

Now I can only be desperate if I know I have nowhere else to turn except to Allah. Desperation is born out of having tried all other avenues. It means I have tried human beings, I took counsel and nobody could help. And most of us who are fortunate have had occasions when we knew we had nowhere to turn, other than back to the direction (*qiblah*) or prayer and to the prayer niche (*mihrāb*) of Allah. The word *mihrāb* is based from Arabic word *harb*, to wage war against falsehood. Falsehood is anything to do with *shirk*. *Shirk*, or association, is our seeing everything other than the light (*nur*) of Allah.

There are shadows in this life. We are shadows. But we can only know the shadow because there is an eternal light (Allah) and that is called, '*The Light of the heavens and the earth*' – the light behind all lights, the light behind all transient and things that change. Allah never changes.

☼   'And you will not find in the way of Allah any change.' [33:62]

The way of Allah, the *sunnah* of Allah, never ever changes. His mercy (*rahmah*) is ever available provided we plug into it. That requires courtesy (*adab*). And the *adab* of that is to have the right attitude of *faqr* – to be truly impoverished to Allah. No matter how wealthy or powerful anybody may be in this world, they are impoverished in comparison with Allah. Every week a president of a country or a very wealthy person is thrown to the dogs. Nothing will last. It is Allah's kingdom. He is the sovereign (*huwa al-Malik*) and we are His servants (*'ibad*). Therefore the courtesy of the *'abd* is to be humble, to expect the best from the King, to know that He (Allah) is the ultimate doer. The prophetic teachings confirm all this by showing us that we are truly sincere when we know that nobody can harm us and nobody can benefit us unless it is by Allah's will. So every other creation is a means. If we expect the best from the source then the rest will be alright. Otherwise we will be in constant fear and agitation about our provision.

Now let us come to modern times. The young people, our young Muslims, will benefit and will take to our *din* fully if they see the benefit of the garden – if they know that worship begins with ablution (*wudu*), which means to stop relating our mind and our limbs to this world, disconnecting from this world. With *wudu'* we are sealed and fit to face our Creator – no more thoughts, no more concerns about our worldly provisions or anxieties, which we all have.

No human being ever comes into this life no matter whom, wretched or a prophet or messenger, without constant concern, but the more our concern is for Allah's sake, the less it will become personalized, and the easier it becomes. The Prophet is described: *'grievous to him is your falling into distress, excessively solicitous respecting you; to the believers (he is) compassionate'* [9:128]. What is he concerned about? That we have no money or bigger houses? He is concerned that we are in this world not yet ready to leave for the next world. How will we be prepared? By perfecting our Islam.

Islam is also based on rituals. The outer rituals will lead to inner awakening. The bowing to Allah, the submitting to Allah ends by prostrating to Allah, and disappearing into His eternal light. That is why we get revitalized by *salāt*, but if it becomes only a ritual without that inner energy within, then it becomes at least some outer manifestation and a gathering. But once our *salāt, sawm, zakat* and *hajj* become confirmed, what are their inner meanings? In this world we are running around from this bazaar to the other, from this job to another, as Hajirah (a.s.) did between *safa* and *marwah*. Our satisfaction lies with trust, faith and abandonment to and freedom in Allah. All of our rituals in Islam have deep meanings. If the young people are educated and taught that, then they will take to our *dīn* because it will lead to their transformation.

First we have to be informed. Then we need to be transformed. The information is that we have to obey to Allah and follow the way of the messenger of Allah (*Rasul Allah*). Then we will find the benefits. Obedience to this path means we are contained and we are in *'aql*. The actual word for intellect or rational mind, *'aql*, itself implies containment. Being contained means not being in a state of dispersion. It is to be reminded of the purpose of our existence. Do we not see that Allah sees us?

So our foundation is *Islām* and *Īmān*. These will lead us to the perfection of *Ihsān*, or perfect conduct. *Ihsān* is the station of *subhanallah* (glory be to Allah). *Subhanallah* – how little we know! *'Lā ilāha illā anta subhānaka inni kuntu min adh-dhālimīn;'* 'There is no god but You, glory be to You; surely I am of those who have wronged [themselves] [21:87]. Allah does not wrong anybody. They wrong themselves. These are the ladders, by Allah's mercy, by which we ascend to Him who is already present here. Allah is forever here, closer to us than our jugular vein, but if our mind is somewhere else then we have missed His presence. Wherever we are, whoever we are, whatever we experience, there is a message in it: to avoid – *la ilāha* –

and then to confirm – *illa'llah*. We avoid that which is evil, whether it is short term or long term, and confirm that which is going to guide us from Allah to Allah, by Allah from our inner state of inner contentment. Inner contentment does not mean we do not continue to struggle. Struggle will continue, but we know that we are doing our best and that is it, without fear or anxiety.

☼　　'Unquestionably, (for) the allies of Allah there will be no fear concerning them, nor will they grieve.' [10:62]

Certainly, those who love Allah have no sorrow. Our hearts are full of love and light and our outer is available to serve as best as we can whoever comes our way. Allah is testing us all the time so we see the extent of our faith and trust in Allah, and the extent to which we have freedom in Him away from the imprisonment of our own limitations.

The foundation of existence is based on Tawhīd.

10: THE MONTH OF MUHARRAM

The universe is governed by cycles, patterns & interconnected
forces. Special (sacred) situations arise as important places or
times in human evolution.

Some twenty odd years ago, I spoke to an enlightened Shaykh in Pakistan who was from Iraq. Shaykh Tahir Alauddin Gilani was the last descendant of Shaykh Abdul-Qadir Gilani (r.a.), the last of that line of an enlightened *silsilah* (chain of lineage) and the head of the *Qadiriyyah*, in charge of the shrine and tomb in Baghdad. He had had to leave because of the atrocities in Iraq, in fear for his life from the threats from the political regime because they wanted him to approve of what they were doing. He was truly a man of Allah.

So he came to Karachi, got married and settled there. I used to visit him whenever I visited Pakistan. Once I asked him what advice he would give to a person like myself, who was from the Middle East and from an Arab background, from countries that had once had tremendous periods of knowledge, light and scholarship, but had now fallen into decay. Since the colonial powers left these places had fallen into deeper colonial bondage in a more invisible way through the banks, money and cultural influences. He advised me to go as far away as I could from the Middle East. At that time I was establishing a centre in Sri Lanka and had even bought land there, but he insisted it was still too close. So I looked at the places with which I was already familiar, including North Africa, Morocco and the Western side of Morocco, but no – they were all too close.

He told me to go away to where the Muslims did not constitute a threat politically, where they were a minority, and were not going to come up with a new thing called 'Islamic Government' and so forth. Then he explained that there would come a period when Muslims would take anything vulgar and wrap around it the name of Islam. He foretold that there would be Islamic banking, Islamic racing and Islamic gambling and so forth. He advised that we had come into a point in our lifetime when we would see the behavior and conduct of many Muslims, especially political leaders, becoming significantly worse.

I share this anecdote because it reflects an awareness of the cyclicality of our experience of existence. Our history is full of events that mark the change in tides that forever influence the conditions of Muslim peoples. The rise and fall of Muslim dynasties and institutions give us so much to reflect upon, not least of which is the unreliability and transiency of this life. And this fleeting nature is the backdrop against which we are all seeking to find our purpose and a steady state of fulfillment – being in this world, but not of it. Cultivating an attuned sense of context is vital to effective action.

The month of Muharram marks the start of the Muslim New Year. It was in this month that Imam Husayn (a.s.) had acted upon the call of thousands upon thousands of people who had been begging him to come to Kufa to represent the Muslims in their bid to restore authority to whomever was the most worthy to lead the Muslim community. It was his responsibility to come and give that which was not his, which was the way of Muhammad. Once ambushed on the plains of Karbala, he offered Yazid's representatives to go far away from Islamic lands, rather than pledge a false allegiance to Yazid. He insisted he had not come there to fight but had been invited. But they would not let him go back.

Three days before the Massacre of Karbala, there came a famous tribal leader who intercepted Imam Husayn and his small group –

mostly women, children and family – and told them, 'Oh grandson of the messenger of Allah! If you go, they will kill you because these people are after power and you are the representative of the all-Powerful. You are not a man who seeks power in this world. You know who you are, but if they kill you, they will not stop killing anybody after that. All other evil acts will become easy.' He replied, 'I want to go back. I want to go to the furthest point of the Muslim lands and teach and be. I am not here to assert anything. Allah is the Creator of this world and these people, and Allah's pattern will eventually prevail because He is the Master of it.' The man added: 'All that I want is to avoid more an more *fitnah* (corruption) amongst the Muslims.' So the Imam replied: 'I have no option and probably they will take that which is in me [meaning his heart] and if they do that, the Arabs will become despised throughout the ages until such time that the entire world despises them and looks down on them.' These were the (paraphrased) words of Imam Husayn (a.s.) in response to the man's concerns regarding his well being.

Imam Husayn (a.s.) was an Arab and so was our glorious Prophet. But this story is not about Arabism. It is about conduct. We entered Jerusalem as Muslims; we were kicked out as Arabs. We entered Andalusia as Muslims; we were kicked out as Arabs. Why did Islam in Andalusia not continue while it continued in the subcontinent? In those days there were small kingships, feudal systems. As soon as an Andalusian embraced Islam he had to be subservient to an Arab. This was the system: they created a ruling elite. Saddam's rulership in Iraq was the same at multiple levels – the political party level, the security apparatus level, the army level, and his own clan level. It is not a small thing. Elitism had reasserted itself.

Taqwa is to be cautious of Him Who is in charge. We do not know how long we are going to last in this world. '*Ittaqi*' is invoked often in the *Qur'ān* as a warning to be cautious. We must look where we are going and be concerned so that we remain safe. But from whom must we remain safe? It is from our ego, our own *Shaytan*, our own stupidities and presumptions.

We are going through a time in the world when if we simply want a quick answer to why something is happening, we will be disappointed. We must go back to the foundation of the purpose of life which we, as Muslims, have been given the clear map for by Allah. We have been given the revelation but also a living *Qur'ān* through the life-pattern or *Sunnah* of our glorious Prophet. There is no excuse. A child who messes about when he does not know the way to his uncle's house is forgiven. He may arrive an hour late and is pardoned, but whoever has the map and is able to read and write and yet ends up in one mess after another, one cul-de-sac after another, has less of an excuse. We are accountable. Children sometimes walk on edges and ledges and get away with it. If a young adult tries to do that, he will usually fail. A small child who is not afraid of the law of gravity does a lot of gymnastics and gets away with it and we say angels protect them.

We as Muslims have no excuse other than getting back to the fundamental issue of who are we? Are we ready to leave this world? Are we inwardly content? Are we outwardly in full accountability and doing our outmost in *jihād*, meaning helping, caring and sharing and taking action appropriately? Are we certain that the unseen and the seen meet and there are so many things we wanted to do and you could not do them? Nearly eighty to ninety percent of all our projects come to nothing. Sometimes they actually occupy us more. They even interfere in the remaining ten percent of our space. Allah says in the *Qur'ān*:

☼ '...It may be that you dislike a thing while it is good for you...' [2:216]

We may hate having to go through a certain period of rest or helplessness. We may hate being occasionally snubbed by our family, our wife or our son. It may humiliate us, but it is good for us to realize the matter is in Allah's hand. At best, we are guardians.

> ☼ '...And it may be that you love a thing while it is bad for you.' [2:216]

So many people have come to me and tried to complain about the son whom they loved – and to whom they had given, say, a car but he had crashed it. The son loved the car and showing off, the father wanted to please the son and prove what a great, powerful father he was, and now they are in a mess. The car turned out to be a 'bad' thing. We have to be alert to our intentions, actions and their consequences. It is not only about constancy of *khayr* (goodness) from the direction we think it is. Allah has created good and evil. Allah is not evil, only good. Evil was created for us to be given the apparent freedom to do something evil and also feel sorrow, remorse and regret so that we return to a god-centric awareness, so that we do *tawbah* (turning back to Allah in repentance). Even in the case of having committed and evil act, for the Muslim or the *mu'min* goodness can come out of it because he is now aware that he has made a mistake and does not want to repeat it.

One of the conditions of *tawbah* being accepted is that we do not repeat wrongdoing. We know it has electrocuted us; we suffered for it so we will not do it anymore because we love ourselves. But which 'self' is it in ourselves that we love? Do we love the *nafs-al-ammāra, al-lawwāma* or *nafs al-mutma'inna*? The *Qur'ān* says:

> ☼ 'Return to your Lord, well-pleased...' [89:27-28]

So do we love our souls or our egos? As a child we start loving the ego, which is perfectly in order. For a seven, nine, ten-year-old boy or girl if he or she does not want everything for himself, there is something wrong. He must have appetite. He must want it – 'Give it to me. I want all the chocolate!' But it would be utterly criminal if we were to do the same thing at the age of fifty because by that time we should have grown in wisdom, reflection, *dhikr* (remembrance) and accountability and have decided that we want to be in such a state such we are ready to leave this world whenever our time has come.

The Prophet taught that whoever is truly in *īmān* has no regrets, meaning that whatever action he or she performs has been referenced to the *rūh*. He could not change what has passed. You and I may have a regret because we undertook an action when we were in a hurry and acted wrongly or stupidly. But if we were in awareness, in *dhikr*, then we could not have done anything different from what we had already done because we said *bismi'llah* – in the name of Allah. The outcome does not matter because we acted from the vantage point of integrity: we were one and not two.

If we are only operating from the ego's point of view and its greed, and possibly hurt somebody, then we should come admit our fault and apologize. The desire for more is a natural drive, until we reach such a time as we are able to say, 'No thank you. I do not want more work. I do not want more business. I do not want more money. It is fine. I have enough clothes and Allah has promised that my *rizq* (provision) will come...I must be better than a bird, of whom the Prophet said, *"They leave in the morning hungry and when they come in the evening they are full."'* Trust in Allah. Trust in Allah does not mean we will be lazy. It does not mean we will not think. It does not mean we should not have a basic understanding of business or calculation, but once we start projecting too far ahead and imagining being this new sultan and so on, then we will end up in the same mess. Every week you find a tycoon, dictator or a despot falling from power and nobody learns from it.

The world is going through a major change. A small community in Timbuktu, North Africa, Southern Iran or Turkey or similar place is no longer isolated. 70 or 80 years ago it was possible to be able to go for a month or two away from it all to spend in isolation, in a cave or in *khalwa* (retreat), or in reflection, as all the prophets did. Nowadays wherever you go, you find American Express, the bank, the IMF and every mobile phone company has already been there. But this does not mean that now we give up being Muslims or lovers of Allah, in submission to the truth that we have come in this world in order to know Allah. Do we give up? The values do not change, but the style changes.

The main reason for the rise of the Sufis was because they were a group of wonderful, decent *mu'mins* (believers) and Muslims who found themselves under the tyranny of rulers who were ruling in the name of Islam, but were not true followers of *Rasul Allah*. So they formed small groups of believers with whom to gather and preserve the teachings of self-knowledge and cautiousness on the path.

One of the greatest beings and one of the earliest Sufis, Imam Junayd, never spoke until there were seven barriers between him and the public. Was he depriving the public because he was only in a country of Muslims in Baghdad? Was he depriving them of this high knowledge? We cannot do this today, but he just did not want people to think that they (the Sufis) were seeking secular power without acknowledging and being totally submitted to the spiritual power. That is why he said he wanted layers between himself and the public. Similarly the Sufis ended up being a little bit enclosed, but this is no longer necessary in modern times. The whole thing is open now. The world has changed. Western powers can do anything, anywhere now in terms of social, political and economic arenas, but they cannot touch your heart. Who knows what is in your heart?

If you grow higher and higher in your inner do not be surprised that you may be subjected to a very strong outer poison. This is maybe for your own sake also, to be strengthened by it but if you cannot take it any longer, then do as I did: make *Hijrah*. You have to be honest to yourself.

In this new month of ours at the beginning of the Muslim

New Year, we are discussing different interpretations of worldly power. Muslims continue with their constant dissension. You and I, however, want to experience the sacred and the sanctuary of inner security; otherwise we will end up being skeptics.

The mess we now have in the Muslim world has resulted in the Muslims either becoming nostalgic for a system that was very simple and primitive, which cannot work in a sophisticated world anymore, or abandoning everything. So we have this schizophrenia. We love *Madinah*, we love the people of *Madinah*, we love the Prophet, but we cannot reproduce that model in its exact outer form. Our clothes are different. Our donkeys are different – nowadays they are called BMWs. Our houses are different. So we cannot duplicate it entirely outwardly. Let us concentrate, therefore, on the inner and the outer will begin to change also. We have in the Muslim world, on the one hand, those who simply harp back to a time when things were easy and simple and every neighbor was responsible for every other neighbor. But nowadays you do not even know who your neighbor is, which may be just as well because they may be dreadful people.

On the other hand, those who recognize something is amiss often want to throw everything out – Islam and being Muslims. They become 'modern' and no longer have *iman*. The word *Iman* is from *amn*. *Amn* is to take refuge, peace. *Amīn* is what is reliably trustworthy – it was one of the nicknames of the Prophet. If you have *Iman* it means you trust that there is a purpose in this life and the Creator of that purpose is Allah and that He will show you His ways. So you trust. Young people nowadays are taught science, technology and other things, at universities and colleges but they cannot translate our *dīn* into something usable, having an immediate impact upon their lives. Do not blame your children who do not do *salāt* on time. They have not tasted what you and I have tasted. We have had the opportunity of having uncles and aunts and other people as models. We had shame. We had a lot of socio-cultural habits that no longer exist nowadays.

Fifty years ago a Muslim was brought up all over the Muslim world to be self-effacing. If you were sitting and eating with the elders, you would not put your hand out too far. You would eat only from what was in front of you, lower your eyes and avoid looking at their mouths. Which teenagers are taught this nowadays? In the canteen they shove things down their throats. In college or university when they eat, they run, walk and spit. Have pity on them. A youngster needs to be taught that life and living is about quality of the mind and body – 'Control your mind. Do not be affected by the half-naked girls all over the place. Concentrate on your studies. Enjoy your gym work.' If he or she knows that by grooming their mind they will do well in their exams, they will do it.

There is no better way I know in grooming the mind than performing *sajdah* (prostration) properly. If you perform *sajdah* properly, you are mind-*less*. If you are mind-*less*, then you are soul-*ful*. So all of our *dīn*, all of our practices, have within them *haqiqah*: the truth, and the truth is the light, which is in your heart. You have no access to a truth except through the *rūh* and the *rūh* dwells in your heart. Therefore, if the heart is pure, you are more and more purified and more and more illumined and less and less suffering from ignorance.

This is Allah's little kindergarten. Do not be saddened. First, we must discover ourselves and change ourselves, and that will come through the *Qur'ān*. There is no doubt in Allah's book of creation: Allah is the perfect Creator. Everything is according to a measure. There is no doubt about His perfection. We can only do what we can, for so many things are not in our hands. Sometimes we do what we can but it turns out to be the worst thing to have done. So we must constantly beseech Allah: *'You know all, I know very little, tell me what I need to know.'* That is why we call upon *al-'Alīm*. If we do not know ourselves as ignorant, we will not be admitted to the courtyard of *al-'Alīm*.

We start with humility. We admit: 'I am forgetful. Allah never forgets. I am mean. Allah is the most generous and may He cover me by his generosity.' And that is the meaning of *astaghfiru'llah*. We ask Allah to cover our lower tendencies and shadows by His perfect light.

'O Mankind, what has deceived you concerning your Lord, the Generous?' [82:6]

II: KARBALA – A METAPHOR FOR THE BATTLE FOR TRUTH

Our lives are sometimes like battlefields between the forces of good or evil. In the long run goodness will prevail.

We are going through exceptionally confusing and difficult times. Whatever we see, whatever we hear, has within it a message of conflict, difficulty, uncertainty and confusion. There are at all times positives and negatives, knowledge and ignorance, life and death, the seen and the unseen meeting. Allah reminds us of this regularly in the *Qur'ān*; if you are a true believer then you have full trust and faith in the unseen and you deal with the seen. You do not deny physicality or material existence. If you deny that, the spiritual side will not be effulgent or clear to you.

We are living at a time now where there is a lot of confusion. During periods of upheaval and change, either a lot of good comes out of it or equally there is the potential for a lot of dreadful and undesirable things to emerge. During times of war and conflict those who are in love with money can make a lot of it through monopolizing food or water supplies – a bottle of water in Baghdad now sells for five thousand dinars. In the late fifties my father had a house with five bedrooms which he sold for three thousand dinars! This just shows you how things have turned upside down. Nearly two to three million people in Iraq are on the edge of malnutrition and many of them are mentally retarded because they have not been fed sufficiently at an early age when the brain grows the most. This is a country which was once one of the wealthiest in the Middle East.

For a few months of war, the first amount requested from the US Congress for the war in Iraq was seventy five billion dollars. Can you imagine how much that is? If you also look at the opportunity that we now have globally you will understand the other side of the story. The opportunities are enormous for us human beings to collectively wake up to the purpose of life. What is this journey of life? What is the meaning of existence? How is it that every one of us is different genetically, in shape, color or background, and yet every one of us is the same? We all want happiness, contentment, certainty and we all want inner peace. How do you resolve this apparent conflict that outwardly no two are the same but inwardly everybody is potentially the same?

Happiness is based on contentment. Contentment cannot occur unless it is based on knowledge, and knowledge cannot occur unless you and I have suffered from ignorance.

Look at Allah's incredible ways. The situation we are all caught in is akin to that of Karbala. Karbala is a blend of *karbun wa balā'*. *Karb* is affliction, difficulty, oppression. *Balā'* is also another word used extensively in the *Qur'ān*, which means worn out, afflicted, tried, from *baliya*, to wear down or wear out. When we Muslims will wake up to our hypocrisy, so many things we took for granted, and the assumptions we made, the rest of the world will also awaken to the true meaning of Islam.

I have personally discovered that if we criticize ourselves and look back and review where we as human beings and Muslims have gone astray, it is not what we did wrong that matters as much as what we did not do right. We did not develop a humane global culture. We took it for granted that we are the same as during the first seventy, eighty or ninety years of the effulgent early period of Islam.

When the Arabs went into Andalusia on the back of the Berbers a situation emerged in which if you did not pay allegiance to an Arab you could not survive in Andalusia. Christian leaders in Andalusia who embraced Islam had to be subservient to Arabs; and therefore we were driven out as Arabs. Look at the Arabs now: how despised they and their leadership have become. They have become the laughing stock of the world. Instead of us Muslims being proud of these twenty-two so-called Arab-Muslim countries, we hide in shame when we see their pomposity and hypocrisy. They constantly say that they outnumber Israelis and yet in their sacrifice (*himmah*) they are the least of the least.

There is no point in our dwelling on a catalogue of catastrophes and feeling miserable. Here is an opportunity for us all, Muslims and others, to wake up and bring back the original spiritual content of the *dīn*. We have made of our *dīn* a great deal of tradition, habit and ritual, all of which are good but if the spiritual light is not central to it, before it and above it, then it is out of balance. It becomes ideas and aspirations without being fully integrated by enactment based on the original Prophetic flowering in which we children of Adam (*bani Adam*) are caught by Allah's design. We are in this world to be ready for the next world. We have come from the world of the unseen, returning to it after we give up that which does not belong to us, i.e. our bodies. Our senses, inner mind and intellect are nothing other than a small window into the eternal garden – this is the message. If we are living it then every believer is happy inwardly and outwardly; he or she is doing their best to serve with no expectations, with no anger, rancor or suicidal nonsense.

There are three major terms in the *Qur'ān* describing trouble and affliction. We already referred to one which is *balā'*. The idea behind the verbal root *baliya* is to put to the test, to try, warn, decline, disintegrate, to be mindful and to take into account. The Arabic language is very rich in that one word can have many meanings. That is why each time *balā'* is mentioned in a verse of the *Qur'ān* it means something slightly different:

☼ 'Every soul must taste of death and We test you by evil and good by way of trial; and to Us you shall be brought back.' [21:35]

The question is to what do we return? You return to the One and Only. From the One comes two. From the two comes multiplicity: millions and millions of people – yet we are the same. The one thing we are looking for is the same. We are looking for constant, reliable happiness, but everybody does it in their own way and that is the meaning of the saying that there are as many ways to Allah as there are human beings. Outwardly we are different, but inwardly we are the same. Who does not want to have constant inner joyfulness and happiness?

Allah says *And We test [afflict] you by evil and good by way of trial.'* For instance, a sudden amount of money may come your way. It will bring you a lot of trouble: all your friends will be jealous and your family will try getting their hands on some of it let alone alerting the taxman! So what appears to be 'good' has within it also the possibility of 'evil' and vice versa. Allah tells us that there are things that we want to have which could be bad for us.

☼ 'It may be that you dislike a thing while it is good for you, and it may be that you love a thing while it is bad for you. And Allah knows, while you do not know.' [2:216]

You do not know because what we want is that which is durable, what is going to last. There is no use in having a minute of pleasure and paying for it with ten years of regret.

☼ 'And We will most certainly try you with somewhat of fear and hunger and loss of property and lives and fruits; and give good news to the patient.' [2:155]

It is not all about our having an easy time. What is easy can be difficult and what is difficult can be easy. The Prophetic teaching is: 'Do not enter a door unless you know clearly how to get out again.' Do not enter into a deal unless it is easy for you to extricate yourself from it.

☼   'Surely We have made whatever is on the earth an adornment for it, so that We may try them (as to) which of them is best in deed.' [18:7]

The best action is the action with no expectation. Do it for Allah's sake. Otherwise, it will be more and more for your selfish sake and you will suffer.

The nature of the human being is that he is in trial and affliction. All of us have 'Karbala' in our hearts. It is not about a place. It is about the battle between that which is permanently good in the way of Allah and that which is to do with the *dunya*.

From a very early stage in our history we Arabs became secular. We had sultans and kings, most of whom were despicable, but we covered it up, saying, 'He is ours and we have to follow'– *ulū'l-amr*. This does not mean he who rules you. It means he who has the authority and qualities to be appointed Leader (*amīr*). We do not translate *ulū'l-amr* simply as being the sultan. For centuries, we did not allow ordinary people to voice their grievances, to speak out, to have freedom of speech. And this is the end of it. So *balā'* expresses part of the nature of existence. *Thawbun bāli* means a dress that has been worn threadbare. The wearing out erodes the resistance of the ego-self, making it easier for us to turn to Allah.

Another term used in the Qur'ān is *fitnah*: *'ahasiba'n-nāsu an yutraku an yaqūlū āmannā wa hum lā yuftanūn'* – 'Does man think [Allah's love and *rahmah* is not such] that they will be left alone to say I trust or I have faith and they will not be tested and tried?' [29:2]

At the time the verse was revealed *fitnah* originally meant testing a coin to know how much gold there is in it. Hence *dinārun maftūn* meant a dinar or a golden coin that had been already proven to be gold. Other meanings of *fitnah* are being subject to temptation, trial, seduction, charm, allure, enchantment and to be captivated. The Arabic name for temptresses is *fātinah*, which means she who will captivate you and try you by her hold over you. *Fitnah* also means torment and trial. What is it you really want? Is it money or power? Or is it to serve in the way of Allah so your heart becomes tranquil? To be infatuated is to be in *fitnah*. To be crazed or to become mad is *fitnah*; if you look at any dictionary, the translation for *fitnah* is discord, strife, or enticement.

The world is such that it will entice us so that we make a choice. Do not deny the *ard*, but deny the *dunya*. *Ard*, meaning earth, is neutral: walk on the earth, eat from the earth, enjoy the earth, but *dunya* is that which draws close to you and connects with your lower self. You begin to say: 'Why not? Don't tell anyone.' This is where we fall. We lose the connection with our *rūh*. The *nafs* thereby becomes distanced from the *rūh*.

> ☼ 'And fear an affliction which may not strike those of you in particular who are unjust; and know that Allah is severe in requiting (evil).' [8:25]

If I am causing trouble in my house and you are my neighbor, be cautioned. This fire that I have lit in my house will also hit you. In the world of easy communication and globalization, any trouble that occurs anywhere will affect the rest of the world. We may not be sensitive enough to it because we are too engrossed in what is right in front of us. So Allah tells us to be careful and not to say that it does not concern us, for it may come to us.

This is what has happened to the Arabs. Look at the hypocrisy: Allah says do not say that it does not concern you. It <u>will</u> come upon our heads. Be wary. Be cautious. We do not know Allah's plans. Allah's plan is to test the extent of our inner reliance on Him and our inner trust that this world is only a place of learning, or a passing phase for us to wake up to the true knowledge that there is only one Creator and from Him have come infinite varieties of creation worshipping Him – most of the time perversely. Every movement of an ant is worship: they scurry around in order to perpetuate their colony and so forth. Everything in existence is an act of worship of the perfect attribute of Allah, the Eternal, the Ever Living, the All Powerful, the All Knowing, the All Forgiving, the All Generous. Every act is worship. If you and I are worshipping correctly, pointing to the ultimate *Qiblah*, which is the light of Allah, then that worship will give us full nourishment. If not then it is a strange kind of worship. It may at least have saved another part of the world and given an hour or so of peace so that we have a bit of comfort in the mosque to worship and others are saved from our tyranny or our hypocrisy.

Every act is worship: *'I did not create the jinn or mankind except to worship.'* [51:56]

This means everything is in worship, but many a time it manifests in a perverted form. Now again with *fitnah*:

> ☼ 'And know that your property and your children are but a trial, and that Allah is He with Whom there is a mighty reward.' [8:28]

Wealth and family can be a distraction and *fitnah*, but the *fitnah* could also be a useful one if it propels us towards awakening. If we pursue such things in the way of the higher by asking Allah to be blessed with children or friends or wealth, their presence can often become a great trial. We can turn that which appears to be trouble into goodness by Allah's mercy. We can turn our sickness, for example, into a higher awareness of what we have needed and how we have abused ourselves.

☼   'Now surely the friends of Allah – they shall have
no fear nor shall they grieve.' [10:62]

This is because they see that Allah is the source of whatever
happens to them. If we know that what Allah does to us is His direct
doing without our necessarily having done anything wrong, then it is
perfection upon perfection. Then our hearts are always tranquil. We
can say, 'I have a sickness and it is a mercy upon me. I was abusing my
body,' or 'My son is running away from me. I became too possessive
of him, had too high expectations of this young fellow – he has to go
through his own experiences.' From this vantage point we only see
goodness.

If it were otherwise, how do you explain the verse: '...and My
mercy encompasses all things; so I will ordain it (specially) for those who
guard (against evil) and pay the wealth tax, and those who believe in
Our signs' [7:156]. How can we explain it if we do not see the rahmah
in every situation? If we do not it is because we are not sensitive
enough and confused – I have a project and I am only concerned
about this project, forgetting that I am Allah's project!

Then this word also appears in the Qur'ān when Prophet Mūsa
(a.s.) comes back and finds all his people have gone astray. He had
appointed his brother Harūn (a.s.) to be their leader and had gone
for 30 days. He was then inspired to stay for 40 days. He returned to
a mess; grabbing Harun by the head, nearly dislodging it because he
was very strong. Two clear verses in the Qur'ān describe this event.
As he was about to cut or cause injury to Harun, he suddenly realizes
what he was doing and says:

☼   'So when troubling adversity afflicts a man he calls
upon Us; then, when We give him a favor from Us, he says:
I have been given it only by means of knowledge. Nay, it is
a trial, but most of them do not know.' [39:49]

As we all know, whenever something untoward happened, our Prophet used to say, 'al-khayrū fī mā waqa'a', that is, 'there is goodness in what has happened.' The implication is to learn from it. Take a lesson from it, but do not repeat it. As he was grappling with the head of Harun, he suddenly saw the light of Allah emerging, and declares that this is Allah's plot to test him to see if he is engrossed in the project of prophethood or in serving him. He then lets go of Harūn and falls ill; his enemies come to treat him and then become his closest friends. We can never know the outcome.

☼   'He brings forth the living from the dead and brings forth the dead from the living, and gives life to the earth after its death, and thus shall you be brought forth.' [30:19]

We do not know what Allah's plot is. Our job is to do our best to be on the path, on the map, to know the map, the path and the atlas that saves us from falling and causing injury and death and being tuned in *dhikr* of Allah's presence. Our job is *'ibādah*. Our job is obedience to the code of Allah.

The third word in the *Qur'ān* about punishment is *'adhāb*. *'Adhb* means pure. The Arabic word is sweet, agreeable, fresh – *ma'un 'adhbun* is sweet water. If water is turbid and has mud in it, you need to filter it. You need to do something to take away the turbidity. That act itself is to shake it. So *'adhāb* therefore comes to mean: to torment, to suffer, to be harassed or to have pain. Muddy water will be 'pained' by the purification process and so will we. When my mind is disturbed and distracted, it needs to be shaken by events, discord and confusion, so that it will reach its accord. I have selected a few verses from the *Qur'ān* for you, which have the word *'adhāb*:

☼ 'And among men is he who says: We believe in Allah; but when he is persecuted in (the way of) Allah he thinks the persecution of men to be as the chastisement of Allah; and if there come assistance from your Lord, they would most certainly say: Surely we were with you. What! is not Allah the best knower of what is in the breasts of all creation?' [29:10]

Afflictions and difficulties are occasional events that will pass, but from which we can derive lessons and insight. We should not get confused and think Allah is punishing us. That is ignorance – like those Arabs who ran after Saddam proclaiming him to be the glory of the Arabs. Now he has humiliated them. If you look to a human being to give you honor (*'izzah*), then he will also mete out humiliation to you (*dhillah*), because *'al-'izzatu li'llāhi jami'an* - 'All glory only belongs to Allah alone'.

Why should a so-called Muslim wage war against a neighboring country? The West told Saddam that they could not back him, but they told him to defend himself so he attacked Iran and they then backed him to the hilt. That is why he became so arrogant because he had the full support of the West. And we simple folk trusted them. When in 1991 Bush senior said to the Iraqis they must rise now, the poor people rose and within a few weeks over a quarter of a million of the best quality young people were slaughtered in Iraq and nobody said a thing. It is only now that some of the more intelligent westerners are admitting that people do not trust them anymore – quite rightly.

What sort of misleading leaders have we had? How close were they to the Prophet? If you love 'Umar, how many of these leaders would he love and hug and acknowledge? If you love 'Ali, how many of them would he acknowledge as his representatives? Shame upon us! However, we do not admit it and therefore that is where we end up because we deny our stupidity, arrogance and hypocrisy.

Our job is to review ourselves and get back to the path. Allah repeatedly says in the *Qur'ān* that we will have trouble so that we may <u>return</u>. Allah's mercy is always present and there is no distance between that and us. There has never been any distance. Where is it in existence that the Light of Allah is not? But we persist in looking somewhere else, so Allah says: '...*Taste then the chastisement because you disbelieved'* [6:30]. It is not because of what you have been doing. You and I are not being punished because we have gone astray. It is by having gone astray that we will punish ourselves! Allah says, '*Wa ma dhalamnāhum wa lākin kānū anfusahum yadhlimūn',* i.e. *'...and Allah is not unjust to them, but they are unjust to themselves'* [16:118].

☼   '...and We overtook them with chastisement so that they may return' [43:48]

They return to what? To humbleness, to the recognition that, at best, we do not know, but we know Him Who knows, Who will give us what we need to know at a time we need to know.

Another *āyah* on *'adhāb*:

☼   'As for those who deny the truth, I will punish them with a severe punishment, here and in the hereafter...' [3:56]

If we deny this truth that everything is passing and yet we are seeking that which never changes, then we will be in great *'adhāb*, in the dark shadows of ignorance.

☼   'And Allah does not bring punishment to people, nor will He, if they are constantly asking Him to cover their faults.' [8:33]

This is the meaning of *istighfār*, or seeking forgiveness. *Ghafara/yaghfiru* is to cover. They say no day passed without the Prophet constantly calling for forgiveness of covering of faults – 'O Allah, cover my faults, cover my weaknesses, cover my forgetfulness, Allah in your infinite knowledge cover my ignorance.'

The so called 'I' is only a shadow of Him who has given us the light in our hearts as a *rūh*, so we realize it is only shadow play. This world is like a dream and the truth is perfectly eternal, which is imprinted in our *rūh*. If we let the self be completely subservient to the *rūh* then we will experience it as *rūhun wa rayhān* – mercy and sweet abundance. Then we are relieved, if not then we are deceived.

Allah's mercy is always there for whoever recognizes that we have deceived ourselves and beseeches Allah to accept his *istighfār*. Thus he is refreshed all the time in his attitude. We should not have these assumptions and presumption that we are always right. We should recognize when we are wrong and apologize. We Arabs are especially vengeful and revengeful; we never forget. That is why we do not admit failure. But whoever does not admit failure will never have access to victory. If we do not recognize our failures, we will not have victory by Allah. Allah wants the Muslim to be victorious, but there is often a big gap between the Muslim and Islam. The reason Islam has not spread throughout the world is because we Muslims have been deficient in our full absorption and transformation by our *dīn*. We have information– and often information overload – and competition between people who have gathered information because they have not been transformed. The Prophetic teaching is that, 'You cannot pass something on which you do not possess.' We do not have resonance with it. That is why in the West more and more people are discovering *tawhīd* without the *dīn*. They are discovering the One behind multiplicity but here we Muslims do not live by the light of the One.

I am exaggerating the sickness we are in so that we can willingly take the remedy. For hundreds of years we have not deserved to live fully as followers of *Rasulu'llah*, but the opportunity is there all the time and I think the current situation gives us the best of opportunities. We Muslims have inherited many good qualities – tremendous qualities of generosity, for example – but not enough rationality, not enough reasoning, not enough acceptance of others and not enough acceptance of criticism. We shut it out and refuse to acknowledge that we make mistakes. We are human beings, after all, and Allah is All-Forgiving. If we recognize this, we can move more quickly into the zone of transformation.

Goodness is like knowledge: it cannot come about unless you and I have suffered from ignorance.

12: THE VICTORY OF KARBALA

*We like to celebrate success & progress. Individually &
collectively we like to remember what was good for us materially
as well as morally.*

Existence in this life is based on cycles and opposites: life and death,
ups and downs, health and illness, this world and the next world, hard
and soft, bitter and sweet, success and failure, and so on. On the day
of Karbala we remember the ultimate success and the ultimate victory
of truth over evil and light over darkness, for the ultimate purpose of
creation in this world is to rise above the frivolous fantasies of human
beings. On this day we remember the call and ultimate success that
came about through the Muhammadi reality as manifested through
Imam Husayn.

Allah says in the *Qur'ān*: '... *I will create a vice-gerent on earth
[Adam as a khalifah],*' [2:30] – which means as a representative of the
truth, in the apparent non-realized light of His presence. There is no
place or situation that Allah has not already designed, or controlled.
He is below or above it, within it, before it, and after it. The entire
creation is founded upon the essence of *tawhīd* (unity). As human
beings we experience actions and try to make sense out of events.
This is called *tawhīd* of manifested situations. We realize that behind
events are the meanings and reasons. It is not the indifference of your
wife that made you upset; it is that you were trying to please her but
failed. See the meaning behind the form whilst progressing towards
the inner core of what appears to be solid matter.

In truth, there is no such thing as solidity. If we look at the insides of molecules and atoms, we will find vast spaces. It appears solid, so that there is for us a little platform for us to take off from into the unseen that has brought it about. Allah says: *'Those who believe in the unseen'* [2:3]. We are the people who believe in the 'unseen' and the fact that the 'seen' is like the tip of the iceberg. There is a much greater hidden force that controls this physical manifestation. To remember Imam Husayn (a.s.) is to remember the spiritual heritage of mankind. It is to remember the purpose of the creation of Adam. It is to remember the gifts of prophethood and our Prophet Muhammad. It is not about emotional outpouring, or witnessing the right and the wrong. It is about celebrating our *dīn*, our rituals, our day-to-day *salāt*, our *sawm*, our *zakāt*, our *hajj*, our *'amr bi'l-ma'rūf*. These are all celebrations of avoiding evil, encouraging ourselves and realizing the great joy and benefit within ourselves and others for doing the right thing.

Ultimately, the right thing is based on the knowledge that there is none other than He – there is none worthy of worship except Allah. And if that is made manifest, then the perfection of it is that Muhammad is our messenger. And if we accept that, then we have to accept his family and righteous companions. We have no option other than to love those whom he loved. The Prophet's boundless love for his grandsons, Hasan and Husayn, was beyond question and is well known by all Muslims. If we look in any of our history books and traditions, there are dozens and dozens of occasions in which the blessed Prophet expressed such an immense love for these two that he called them *'Sayyidan shabab ahlu'l-jannah'* – they are the masters of the youths in the garden. *'Shabab'* in Arabic means youthful, because in the garden, *insha'Allah*, we will regain the meaning of youthfulness, which means possessing full energy and full vitality to absorb the full glory of paradise.

There are so many incidents, from their birth until the departure of the Prophet, that tell us of the deep, profound transmitive – not just emotional – love of the grandfather towards his grandchildren. As we know, the Prophet did not have living sons of his own, so these children were the equivalent of that, from his most beloved daughter Fatima Zahra (a.s.). There were so many occasions on which they would ride on his back, and he would enjoy it, and later he would put them on his lap and talk about it. Once one of his wives has a very disturbing dream and came to him and said: 'Oh *Rasūl Allah*, I saw a piece of you coming into my room here, and I am most disturbed.' This story is related in many of the *Sihah* (canonical collections of *hadith*), including Tirmidhi and many others. So he said to her: 'This is great news. There will come a part of me in the form of Husayn into this world.' Within a year or so Fatima (a.s.) gave birth and when she brought the young baby into the room the Prophet reminded her that this was the manifestation of the dream.

The Prophet had many incredible unveilings and revelations regarding future events, concerning how his own people would cause the martyrdom and slaughter of many members of his own family. It is narrated that on the specific occasion when the Prophet said 'Part of me will come into this room,' he turned aside and tears were seen coming out of his eyes. When asked the reason, he said that he saw some of their own people shedding his blood and Jibrael (a.s.) had just given him a handful of the sand of Karbala saturated with his blood. These are the times that we Muslims recall and remember, because without remembrance there is no transformation.

Allah enjoins upon us in the Qur'ān: *'Therefore do remind, surely reminding does profit. He who fears will mind, And the most unfortunate one will avoid it, Who shall enter the great fire; Then therein he shall neither live nor die.'* [87:9-13]

We are reminded about what is useful. It is useful because we are given information that moves us. The candle gets the information that it is to be lit, and it will give light. Otherwise, it is useless –

mere information overload. It is therefore enjoined upon us to mark any specific occasion through which we remember him. I recall one man whose glorious inner joy and effulgence amazed me, and when I asked him about his practices – which Sufi *tariqah* he was with and who his teachers were – he said, 'No one, nothing, nothing at all. The only thing that I do is that I always remember the thirst of Imam Husayn whenever I drink water.'

We must use any means to be shaken out of our lethargy. The *nafs* of the human being is the veil that separates the eternal ever-present, ever-effulgent light of Allah. So any occasion that shakes us out of our forgetfulness, our distractions, our fantasies, our anxieties about our *rizq*, or reputation – is an aspect of worship. It is related that one of Imam Husayn's (a.s.) last battle cries was: '*O let that which is between You and me be a perfect connection, and that which is between me and creation be in ruins.*' It means that if we know Allah thinks well of us because we are truly in total and utter obedience, then let other people think what they want to think of us, because it does not matter. These are the basic, fundamental stepping stones of our remembrance of our glorious Imam.

It is also an occasion for immense sadness. Indeed, in the cosmic configuration too, there is sadness. Most people, even if they are not in Islam, even if they are not lovers of *Ahlu'l-Bayt*, feel the constrictions of Muharram. It continues until about the 11th day and then there is relief. Relief in which sense? In *Haqq* – in that all belongs to Allah, that the *rūh* of Imam Husayn has returned to Him Who had it from its beginning to its end. It allows the unveiling of truth, not the false idea that we can do something because we have a little power, money, or lust, or Machiavellian cunning like Muʿawiyah and Yazid. The commemoration and the remembrance are for us firstly to be saddened that we are not with Husayn and that we have not completely taken on that light upon our own candle. Then there is the celebration and the wonderful joy we must have in that we as Muslims have examples like the glorious Prophet coming before us, rekindling the same spirit of fearlessness in the way of Allah, uncompromising in the way of Allah, showing gentleness with the poor and destitute, complete and utter humility and steadfastness.

The Prophet said, 'Husayn is from me and I am from Husayn.' We as human beings can understand 'Husayn is from me' at many levels. The very basic level of understanding this saying is linguistic and biological – that this person has come from me because he is the child of my daughter and the child of beloved Imam 'Ali. So we know he is from him physiologically, mentally, and in all respects. It is said that Imam Hasan (a.s.) resembled the Prophet up to his chest and in the bottom other half Imam Husayn resembled the Prophet in every detail. So we understand that he has come from him. But what about the second half of his statement: '...and I am from him?' Who is the prophet, apart from the biological being Muhammad *ibn* Abdullah, and so on? What is the meaning of the word 'prophet'? What is the reality of our glorious Prophet? What did he represent? He represented the truth that we as human beings have to completely acknowledge that Allah is our *Rabb* by being *'abd*. By submitting, by being in *'ibadah*, in obedience and in full faith that all is well because it is under His tent, and we have come by Him, we are going to be guided by Him, and we will return to Him.

We all love the Garden and we hate the Fire. How do we achieve the Garden? By not doing wrong. By being in constant contentment with whatever we are given, by being in *shukr* and *hamd*, and whenever we are not, by being in *sabr*; when we have, to give; when we don't have, being in greater contentment that we will not make more mistakes and get into more difficulties. This is the way of Muhammad, and this is the way of Husayn (a.s.). Husayn would re-enact the same thing in full – if you like – the same 'drama' in a sense of total and utter submission and martyrdom.

Muslims go into constriction during the months of Ramadān

and Muharram. If you want expansion, go for constriction. If you want to know wealth, accept poverty. If you want to know health, realize the constant possibility of illness. If you want friendship, realize that you are alone, and then you will find that everybody is your friend. The law of opposites is unchangeable. Everything lies in its opposite.

The Prophetic teaching is: everything that goes beyond its limits reverts to its origin. So it is the same thing with the arrogance of the Arab leaders within 60 years after *hijrah*. Imam Husayn's martyrdom was in the year 61 AH (ca. 680 CE). His first seven years were in the lap of the Prophet, until the departure of the Prophet and his freedom from the prison of this world. Then he continued his life with his blessed mother and father. When his father departed, he was 37 years old. There was another 10 years with his beloved brother Imam Hasan (a.s.). The Prophet described Hasan and Husayn are the most glorious leaders whether they stand or whether they sit; whether they are in this life, or whether they are not, in that they are examples for us to take upon ourselves, to live as though we are with them, and worthy of being with them. This is to do with transmission. There is no point in our just glorifying them and weeping over them, or acknowledging the greatness of our Prophetic examples, unless we genuinely want to be among them. So the secret is for us to visualize it, love it, abandoning ourselves to those profiles, so that we can be resurrected in this life as being amongst them. If we deserve it, we will feel it. We will know.

How else can we behave other than remember that we are accountable to these beings, to the Prophetic path, to the *din* of Islam and to the *Shari'ah*. Whoever thinks he knows will end up by Allah's glory humbled by ignorance. Call upon Allah from the point of ignorance for He is the All Knowing. And Allah in His glory and His mercy will constantly put us at the level of helplessness, so we call upon His help, not knowing which way to turn, so that we call upon

Him as the Guide, the Life-giver, the Returner, the Ever-providing, the Bestower, the Compeller.

These are the examples we need to live by during the time of the constrictions of Muharram. The constrictions of Ramadān lead to the celebration of Eid. Eid is returning to our habits. It is from the Arabic word 'ādha/ya'udū – to return to apparent normality – or in the case of many of us to our normal heedlessness, not thinking how, when and what. So the constrictions of Ramadān lead us to Eid, and the constrictions of Muharram lead us to glorify and celebrate having had this glorious being who truly lived the dīn of his grandfather. Had he not lived our dīn, it would have vanished. It would have become nothing other than the practices of kings and sultans, as we witness nowadays. In the name of so and so, more and more grand mosques are being built. More buildings and highways are being built to glorify various rulers, but there is no submission and no tearful eyes, no love for the poor, the miskīn, the destitute. If there was any destitution, it was on the 10th of Muharram. The most glorious family in existence was rendered destitute.

Look at the behavior and conduct of this noble man: There were 30,000 fighters surrounding his tiny camp. All that night they dug channels around the tents to stop the intruding enemy. If it were any of us, we would probably have submitted and fled. To the last minute, this being was on his horse going in and out of the battle. There was nobody left, and his sons and other close members of his family were brutally and callously slaughtered. It is not just about comparing evil with goodness, it is about seeing the actions.

The Prophet says that even if it is the Day of Reckoning and you have in your hand a palm tree, plant it. This is how Imam Husayn (a.s.) 'lived' the dīn. To the last minute, he fought in the only possible way that was allowed to him. By the 4th of Muharram he was on his way and his group were not allowed to return. He was told that he had to pay allegiance to someone who behaved most despicably in human terms. He had come because people had invited him to do so, and promised him support. Those people had now been threatened and bribed and had turned their backs on him. He did not want to shed blood, but he could not go against *Haqq*. How could he have acknowledged something that was inherently evil as being right? It was not possible for him.

These are the multiple, infinite lessons of the martyrdom of Imam Husayn (a.s.). Therefore, we have to celebrate the victory of truth. It is not just about the shedding of blood and feeling a bit sad. We should feel sad about ourselves for not being a hundred percent forthright and being more concerned about our reputation and our hypocrisy. Imam Husayn (a.s.) left Makkah just before Hajj, just before the standing at *'Arafat*. Everybody was shocked. This was the time of Hajj and he who was the most glorious person had left them. When he had declared his *Imamate* people acknowledged him as the most worthy being to be followed. Yet he left with only a small band of people – a few of his family and close followers. He tried constantly to encourage this small band of people to return. He told them his enemies were not after them, but after him because he was singing the eternal song of truth – that they could not be led by people who were misleading themselves and others for there would be no Islam left, only a closeted Islam and a bit of a private, personal *'ibadah*, but no society, no *Ummah*. These were the true lessons. The Imam's victory has been the victory of truth which will stand the test of time at all times.

The truth is that none other than Allah rules this world. At best we are His slaves and servants, acknowledging that there is nothing in our hands. If we have anything, it is being lent to us. What are we doing with it? Imam Ali (a.s.) says: 'If what we have earned is *halāl*, then we are accountable for what we did with it.' Why did we only favor our friends and relatives? What about the poor and destitute, and those who are impoverished at heart? Why haven't we reached them? And if it is *harām* then we will be punished – hopefully immediately, so we do not have to suffer later in the Greater Fire.

The victory of Imam Husayn (a.s.) is the victory of every true, transformed believer. It is the victory of all of us as Muslims, in that truth will prevail. If not now, then it will prevail later. I once had the opportunity to find out where the graves of some of the criminals in our history were. In Damascus the Head of Antiquities there told me of the research they had done and the nearest place they could find where all these people were buried, especially the father of them (Mu'awiyah), was about 600 to 700 yards from the Umayyad Mosque, where there was a ladies' public bath. Next to it was a public toilet for ladies. And yet look at the glory and the remembrance of Imam Husayn (a.s.) to be found everywhere today.

I have been privileged to travel extensively in India – North, South, East and West. The Islam that emerged from this sub-continent was effulgent with the love and the example of Imam Husayn (a.s.). There are 400 or 500 centers called *'Āshūrkhāneh* – places to remember *'āshūrah*, the tenth of Muharram and the events that took place on that day, to remember what the meaning of the perfect person is.

The perfect person is he who remembers and acknowledges the perfect Creator. The perfect Creator is exclusive. He is the only Creator. You and I have nothing of our own. Life has come from Him to us for a short while so that we wake up to His presence. That is the perfection of Muhammad and the perfection of the Muhammadi beings, such as the *Imams* and other enlightened beings. They take that profile. It is not personality. It is not a style of life. It is an inner awakening to the perfection that: 'I do not know. But I know He who knows all who will give me what I need to know at the time I need to know it.' Whether it is to fight, or whether it is to stop, or whether it is to remain in this world, or whether it is to leave this world. This is called true security based on your inner *haqīqah*. This is what we glorify about our great *imams* and this is what we, as Muslims, have as the advantage over the others.

We know exactly how Imam Husayn (a.s.) lived. We know what he did. Are we living it? If not we should weep. But we are intending to live it. Then smile inwardly beyond smiles, but also within *shari'ah*. So you end up outwardly *shari'ah*, inwardly *haqiqah*. Outwardly you are in Allah's hand and acknowledging creation, thanking Him and thanking creation, inwardly you are beyond any of the turmoil and disturbances of this life because all of us will experience the departure from this life and freedom from it into the effulgence, eternal light of Allah.

'O human being! Surely you are toiling painfully and continue to struggle until you come to meet your Lord.'
[84:6]

13: THE CURRENT STATE OF PALESTINE

Part of the human struggle is against injustice & oppression. To overcome personal prejudices & ignorance is an important step against injustice.

Allah declares the absolute truth regarding the purpose of this existence, its journey, its beginning and its end. Allah reminds us that if you and I declare that we have faith and trust in the One and Only Creator, Sustainer of it all, we will be shown the extent of our sincerity. The trials and afflictions of life are the catalysts for this self-awakening. The meaning of *fitnah* in Arabic is temptation, trial, discord, sedition. It seduces you away from truth. The verbal root of *fatana* is to try or prove something, in other words, to go to the essence of a matter. If a gold coin had been proven to be true gold, it was known as *dinar maftūn*.

Allah wants us to realize the extent of the truth of what we are claiming. Allah causes existence to become a mirror reflecting our state or condition. If you and I are not unified in our human oneness, how can we have access to the *nūr* (light) of the eternal One? We first have to become unified before we can talk about *tawhīd* (Unity), which is the foundation of existence and the purpose of all prophetic lights and the messages that have come to mankind. It is about the One Source. If we are not focused upon the original light, how can we ever have access to the magnificence of the manifestations of the One? If we are dispersed, then an aspect of us is on this side and another on the other side. So Allah reminds us in this *ayah* not to ever think we are left to our own devices. We will be tested by what we do and experience, by our friends, by our family and by events, so that we know the extent of our *īmān* (faith) in Allah. Do we know that He is in charge now? Do we know that Allah is the doer of it all and we have to read what the meanings of events are and act appropriately? If not, we remain confused. If we are confused, distressed, or at a loss, it is not because of the fault of Islam, or of the prophetic teachings. It is probably because we have not read it properly or applied it – often both! We have the basic parameters of this magnificent path.

Let us examine the atrocities and catastrophic situation that Muslims experience and suffer from due to the injustices that are being perpetrated in Palestine. Massacres, attacks, shellings, deprivations, embargos, land-grabbing, bulldozing & usurpation, harassment the list of persecutions is long. We can make a quick and superficial condemnation of events, which everybody will feel good about because here is obvious injustice and we can rise against it. We can talk about unifying the Muslim *ummah* (nation). We can talk about the 1.5 billion people that could rise up or the possibility of even 1% of them raising their voices sincerely. It would be a far greater force and power than the small number of Zionists, and so on. Or we can look at what Allah's message is to all His creation. Allah says: *'And I created not the jinn and mankind except that they should worship Me (alone).'* [51:56]

Allah's message is to all of creation, not only to the Muslims, or to the unjust and arrogant ones. It is to the whole of mankind, all races and colors telling us when we are disturbing the purpose and peace in this *dunya* (material world). We can simply sit here and argue and curse the Zionists and feel a bit better, or even criticize some of the Muslims who have not protested, or the Arabs or others, but it is not going to do us much good. We must read the full truth of the situation.

It behooves us as intelligent human beings to read the situation properly, to understand the facts of the matter, to know what is going on, and then we will find alternatives as to what we can do.

Let us look at the situation now in Palestine. Since 1946-1947 and the creation of Israel in 1948, every year for the Muslim *ummah* (nation) and the Palestinians is worse than the year before. Sometimes the situation appears to improve, but look at the sum total of it. When Arafat was calling for justice, he got nowhere. But when he wanted to be a President and hero of a country, they gave him the rubbish heap of Gaza, a national anthem and directives to police his destitute people. The economy was based on donations, handouts and earnings from slave labor and casinos.

We must look into the major issue from every angle. What is Allah's intention? Allah's intention is for us to worship Him properly. How can people worship if they do not have the basics of health, shelter, food, security and peace? How can they get to know the ways of Allah? How can they discover their *dīn* (way of life)? How can they live the *Qur'ān* if they are continuously oppressed and disturbed? It is Allah's way, Allah's design and Allah's purpose. As Muslims we are supposed to be reflecting the perfect way.

Soon after the departure of the fourth of the great *Khulafā'* (Caliphs), by the time we enter into the third or fourth decade after *Hijrah* (migration from Makkah to Madinah in 622 CE), we find significant divergences amongst Muslims. These differences culminated in a situation about 500 years ago when the territory of Muslims dominated the world. The loss of Andalusia cut off that ongoing continuous relationship between the East and the West. We Muslims and the rest of the world began to impose barriers to trade and became arrogant so that the goods and products in our lands, mostly in the subcontinent, Mesopotamia, Iran and Turkey and in other parts of the Far East and North Africa, became our monopoly. Eventually Europeans found a way around it with the discoveries of the Americas and the routes to the rest of the world. The short-lived monopoly on trade ended.

Look at the situation of 200 years ago: The Europeans, Jews and Christians from the rest of the world had enclaves in every great Muslim city and even in some of the smaller cities in the Middle East, as well as North Africa, Cairo, Istanbul, Tehran and elsewhere. All of these cities had strong communities of Christians and Jews. Where was the Muslim enclave in Paris or London? There was not even a single *halāl* hotel in London until late in the twentieth century.

It is only possible to give you a few glimpses of how, over the last few hundred years we have been continuously regressing in terms of social, cultural, economic and spiritual development. By that time, the Westerners had separated secularism from religion and made it desirable to accumulate wealth. We also inadvertently separated, in a way, our hearts from our heads. Islam is the path of *tawhīd* (unity). We need to connect reason and rationality with the divine light. We must deal with the outside world with our *'aql* (intellect), with reasoning, with diagnostics, with *shūra*, with counsel and then act with our heart in the way of Allah.

During the last 200 years all Muslim peoples and countries have fallen under the *kufr* way of thinking, their system of education, health, finance, economy, in our business, trade, clothes, houses and in overall style and ways of living. We have been mimicking their ways thoroughly and then suddenly we are desperate and call for *Jihād* (struggle) whilst Arabs are still building their casinos, Disneylands and stock markets.

A few decades ago, young and sincere Muslims from the Middle East were asking their rulers why they were living off *kufr* money (borrowed or unearned) and were not deriving their authority and power from their people? The oil companies were inadvertently puppets of despotic rulers everywhere. Artificial calls for *Jihād* (struggle) were often designed to get rid of ongoing and unsatisfied young Muslims to Palestine and elsewhere so that Arab rulers could carry on squandering the ill-gotten wealth.

We will make no progress if we do not look at the whole situation clearly from its beginning to its end before judging and blaming. Then we can come up with correct ideas and directions. If we do not do anything now we will be in every way accountable. We cannot just sit and talk and blame the past on others. We know there are injustices. We know there are immense abuses; there are untold situations all over the world, especially where Muslims suffer major injustices. Look at what is happening in Kashmir, Afghanistan, Iraq, North Africa and Sudan. Wherever you look there is trouble. And yet we are still talking in terms of independence resulting in another flag, another basket case economy and disagreements between parties mimicking Western democracies. We are taught by our glorious Prophet that there is no way other than dependence on Allah, trust in Allah and following in His ways, helping the *mu'minūn* (believers), not taking others as your friends.

We have learnt the Prophetic traditions, we have more and more *huffaz* (memorizers of the *Qur'ān*), but less and less living of the *Qur'ān*. This is the situation of presumption that we know which leads to hypocrisy. We are the receptacle of the past; we have inherited the outcome of centuries of neglect and fossilized attitudes. Now we are being shocked and woken up by Allah's *rahmah* (mercy) through these catastrophic situations. You see the Israeli cabinet meeting in a simple, modest place, a small room, whereas the Arab rulers meet in ostentatious luxury. Which of these two styles is more Islamic than the other? Human beings are not stupid. We cannot simply say 'Islam' and not live it. We can honestly say that most of us are not following our *dīn* (way of life). For two or three weeks in Hebron, people were under 24-hour curfew. For 3 days people in Hebron were only allowed to go out for 2 hours. There are about 40,000 Muslims in Hebron. It was no longer a case of imprisonment, but total uncalled for brutality. This sort of thing is still continuing in

Palestine while fat, so-called Muslim leaders fly in their luxury jets to useless meetings to make grand pronouncements and take no helpful actions. They may allocate some emergency funds to buy peace but their hearts are dead and their end will also be miserable.

Allah says in the holy *Qur'ān* that: *'Surely Allah has bought of the believers their persons and their property for this, that they shall have the Garden'* [9:111]. It is not enough just to give something that you have in your pocket. Are you giving yourself? Are you giving your time, your energy and your heart? Are you connected? The reason we are in such a miserable state is because we are not connected to Allah's ways and His light of heavens and earth.

Look at the *ahl ul-dunya* (people of the material world) on the other hand! They are equally Allah's creation. The Israelis are now living under immense fear. They fear a young man with a stone in his hand. Allah's *rahmah* (mercy) is everywhere. Allah's *rahmah* is upon us who are suffering from these tragedies for Allah's *rahmah* reaches everyone in every situation. Where is it that Allah's mercy is not? So we wake up to the fact that we all are sons of Adam, and we have to live in this world with utmost *taqwa* (cautious awareness), implying living and enjoining good and justice. It does not mean that we simply sit in the mosque and allow the injustice to take place outside. Are we ready for a true awakening in every step?

The situation now is that the globalization of so-called democracy has swept beyond the ability of any Muslim community to come up with an alternative way of governance. Where in the world is there a place that the Muslims are living in a way that you as a *mu'min*, as a believer, can go and function? We suspect each other. We have all of these different *madhāhib* (schools of law). We only see differences. Where is the love and where is the meeting point with the *Nūr* (light) of Allah? In every small country people are killing each other – take the Comores, for example, where two impoverished islands are attacking each other. You go to Bangladesh, Tanzania and

Nigeria and you will find a similar situation. Wherever we look, in every town and city, we find this faction and that faction and yet we have the audacity to talk about an *ummah* (one nation)! Such rhetoric may make somebody feel a bit better for a minute but it is not a remedy. The remedy is to read the inherited sick situation we are all in and then come up with alternative ways whereby we can act, but in a way that will be sustainable. We need sustainable resistance, a sustainable way of life with humility, and not haughty defiance.

I was a youngster when Israel declared independence. In Iraq they thought it was possible for the Iraqi army alone to crush it, let alone all the other Arabs and Muslims combined. What happened? We defied them with ignorance, without knowledge, competence or evaluation and without being under the banner of Islam. We congregated under the banner of nationalism, false pride and other 'isms'. Then look at the last half of the last century: We had despotic leaders who had either come from the army or from nationalistic backgrounds, professing Islam symbolically, going for a *Jum'ah* (Friday Prayer), but where was their *taqwa* (fearful awareness) and love of truth? Where were their hearts? They were not servants of Allah (*'ibadu'llah*). They inherited the outer dress of their *dīn* without earning it and they were not the representative of *Rasūl Allah* (the Prophet of Allah). Allah expects a true vicegerent to rule in this world, not hypocritical Muslims.

The reason Islam and the Muslims will continue to suffer is because we do not have Prophetic or *'Muhammadi'* leadership. We express love for the Prophet Muhammad, we love his *Sahābah* (companions) and his *Ahl ul-Bayt* (Family of the Prophet) and yet we are far from appropriate leadership. How did 'Umar live? That humble, powerful man slept in a small corner of a mosque with a brick under his head. And look at Imam 'Ali – his way, his demeanor, clothes, sword, his divinely inspired heroism and yet legendary gentleness and clemency. Then there were other enlightened Muslims representing ultimate justice on this earth. They were the true *khulafā'* (caliphs) of Allah. The West separated secularism from religion because the Judeo-Christian path had become obscure and adopted by Constantine in order to enhance and strengthen his empire. Malaysian rulers did a very similar thing 500 years ago. The Sultans introduced Islam to strengthen their rule and make everybody bow down more. Many of our sultans, kings and despots used religion to increase their worldly power, rule and wealth.

We have examples in Andalusia where the Sufis and the others who were bringing people to Islam were attacked by the sultans because they reduced the *jizyah* (tax on non-Muslims) by bringing in people to the *dīn*. They showed up the sultans as not living according to the ways of the Prophet and this was an embarrassment. That is why in so many Muslim homes they prefer to have non-Muslim servants, so that they can carry on their non-Islamic ways in their home rather than be witnessed by a Muslim servant. In Kuwait, many servants were Christians imported from Goa so that they could serve alcohol to their masters. Wherever you look there is sadness and suspicion instead of the believer's heart overflowing with joy. Allah will show us and put the mirror of creation in our face so that we see the truth and stop calling ourselves this and that *madhhab* (school of law), whilst not being worthy of even the glance of the Prophetic light, let alone all the knowledges that we have in our great tradition.

It is no use simply accusing this group or *madhhab* (school of law) and come up with useless, instant and simplistic remedies for complex sicknesses. Look at what happened in the past two hundred years and how the Muslims in Turkey, Egypt, Iran and elsewhere mortgaged their countries and people to European banks. In Turkey, it was over by 1810 when the Sultan had begun to modernize. We have to be modernized all the time, but once we have taken and adopted a *kufr* system, we are already under its hegemony. By 1850 most of the training in the Ottoman army was given by officers from the West, several of them from Austria, France and Britain, because we did not develop and educate our people as the West was doing.

By the time the Suez Canal was built, Egypt was completely under the weight of the debt to the banks. Soon after that, Britain decided to impose direct rule on the country. All the so-called Muslim countries ended under direct control through the banks. In each of these countries, the bankers instituted systems of retrieving the money they had lent. In the case of Turkey, which had a substantial loan, they instituted a committee of bankers (two of whom were Jews) who were living in Istanbul, to make sure that through customs, excise, and other means, these loans were repaid, with an incredible amount of usury and interest. That is why Turkey came to be called the 'Sick Man of Europe', because the sick was not yet dead, as his blood could still be sucked, until the sickness was so great and Kamal Ataturk came to finish it off.

Allah sends *Shaytān* in order for us to wake up to the *Rahman*. Look at Allah's ways. He says in the *Qur'ān*: *'Then which of the Blessings of your Lord will you both [jinn and man] deny?'* [55:13]. Wherever you look if you do not see the *rahmah* (mercy) within it, then you have missed this constantly recurring point. Do not brush aside the difficulty and the challenge. Allah is challenging us all the time. Do we think that we will be left without being tested and afflicted so that we know exactly where our *Jihād* is? *Jihād* is from an Arabic word which means 'to exert energy'. You and I have to exert energy as long as we are alive.

The Prophet (may the peace and blessings of Allah be upon him and his family) has taught us that we are continuously accountable to this light and our higher self. We need to continuously ask ourselves, are we truthful, are we honest, are we aware, are we in *dhikr* (remembrance) of the One? Are we aware we are doing such and such for Allah's sake, by Allah's *rahmah*? Are we ready to leave this world? The inner *Jihād* (struggle) and the outer *Jihād* both connect at all times. But there is a hierarchy. If someone is physically sick then he is in stress and his mind is not clear. Thus, he is not qualified to lead others during this serious disturbance. It is for this reason an ignorant person should not embark upon an action, because that action will mislead people more than benefit them. That is why so many false struggles have been declared and have failed. The danger of involving other people is serious when politics and religion are confused. *Jihād* (struggle) has to continue forever – any minute now we may leave this world, and the Prophet said: *'You will die according to the condition you are in, and you will be resurrected in that condition also.'* So what condition are we in?

Our experience in the grave and beyond will be shaped according to our inner mirror. If the condition and consciousness we were in were the highest possible, then we are on our way to the best destiny ready to meet our Prophet. Outer combative *Jihād* has to be qualified by the enlightened *'ulama'* (religious scholars). There are many conditions for it including the presence of a just and prophetic ruler or king. You cannot have a king sitting in some cozy palace ordering his paid *'ulama'* to go and call for a *Jihād*; the leader must be in the front.

In the Western world, the separation between government and religion resulted in considerable growth and development in their social, political and economic life. As for the 'reformed church', it is constantly being 'de-formed' and fighting for survival. At one church in England where they were selling beer, the bishop was asked how he could justify alcohol in a place of worship. He replied that alcohol is part of the Christian culture. If we are not careful, we will end up having Islamic banks as part of our 'Muslim' culture, and many other *shaytanic* activities as part of our culture.

To return to the point, we must read and understand the present situation as the culmination of decades of our living in spiritual lethargy, ignorance and superstition, under despotic leaders and ignorant *'ulama'*. We are now reaping the result of deviation from original Islam. You cannot simply attack the *kuffar* or Christians whilst they lead globally in most human endeavors. They are the inventors of money, modern arms, information technology and all modern ways of life. Yet, Iraq's government defied the world powers and set itself up for suicide. We have over a million children in Iraq who are mentally retarded. A million and a half of the best people of Iraq and Iran were killed in the senseless war, which was encouraged by Western powers. The truth is that no Muslim country or people have any real independence politically or economically. I was brought up in Iraq just after the Second World War, which had not touched the town I was born in, because we hardly needed imported goods or products. Within twenty years the country's income from oil doubled, the number of poor people increased and self-sufficiency had vanished.

In any Muslim country now, if you cut off the supply of medicines or certain food items for a month or two, you will have serious destitution. The globalization of the *kufr* system and the power of its finance is everywhere. How do we release ourselves from its stranglehold? My reading is that this so-called pseudo democracy, which is un-Islamic, needs to be changed and imposed in a real way. At the moment, our rulers pretend to be just and democratic but they are only able to mimic the West and appease the world powers. The Muslims know that they have to live according to the way of the Prophet, Abu Bakr, 'Umar, 'Uthman, 'Ali (upon them all be peace) and other great, enlightened beings. We know that we are not living anywhere near what is expected. So we end up having this paradox: we love the West and Western ways, and are nostalgic about our *Islam*, which stops at the gate of the mosque.

Where is the *tawhid* (unity) in this? *Din* implies a way of living, a debt upon us for the gift of life. It is a complete code of life. And that is why 'Islam' is the only true path. And that is why we find so many of the so-called religions moribund and incomplete. Gathering in a temple one hour every week is not good enough. Why don't we also breathe only once a day? It is about our functioning, our cells, our mind, our heart and our *rūh*; to be in worship and awe all the time is to be truly in Islam and thus be safe from afflictions of self or society.

We have to be guided by the divine spark within us, which is the *rūh* (soul). Otherwise, life will be difficult and miserable. We eat, sleep, etc. and at the end of it, we are under six feet of dust at best. What is it all about then? As Muslims we have a path which, if lived, would transform everybody and which others would want. But if we are not living it, then that potential joy and knowledge is not achieved. Materially, outwardly, we can see that Muslims have become inferior, because of our negligence. We had at one time all the sciences and an advanced way of life. But often, when the Muslim scientist or scholar died, with him died his creativity and knowledge. When the great physician and philosopher Ibn Sina died, there were a few *hakims* (healers) after him, but a few decades after that nothing was left. His *qanūn*, which is translated as 'canons or rules' was taken by Western medical practitioners and remained their main manual until recent history.

The question arises as to why have we not grown in culture and civilization? In most cases our rulers were not fit to rule in the prophetic sense. They used Islam to oppress Muslims and appointed clergy to confirm their despotic and often inhumane ways. Thus no ongoing institutions for education, health or civil service came about. Our schools offered basic *shar'iah* (revealed laws) and *Qur'ān* recitation – static and unpopular primitive attempts. No history, geography, health, mathematics or any other sciences were taught as they once had been.

We must realize that we have all deviated from the way of the Prophet. It is Allah's *rahmah* (mercy) that we still have the *Qur'ān* intact and that we still have the knowledge and the love of the Prophet in our hearts. These are great foundations to build upon the future of illumined and universal Muslim lives. Everybody wants durable happiness and spiritual reference. But often happiness becomes a disaster for five minutes of pleasure. We must take responsibility for our actions. Expect good destiny and live Allah's perfect ways and decrees joyfully. To live in *taqwa* (cautious awareness) with the goal of knowledge of Allah, following the footsteps of *Rasūl Allah*, is the road to safety and success.

'Do men think that they will be left alone on saying, We believe, and not be tried?' [29:2]

14: LIFE AFTER DEATH

The notion of immortality & the human desire to be remembered after death may give a hint at another phase of consciousness in life after death.

Our life in this world is a journey of discovery. We have come from the darkness of the womb into this world where there are ups and downs, good and bad, happiness and misery, and all the while we all journeying towards another phase – that is, after death. There are essentially three key challenges or issues in everyone's life, irrespective of who we are, whether intelligent, less intelligent, healthy, wealthy, powerful or poor. No matter who we are these three issues remain of paramount importance.

The first is: Who am I? Why is it that at certain times we are happy and at other times we are not? Are we not the same person at all times or are we different from one moment to the next? Why is it that if we are empowered we feel good about it and when we have no power, when we are ill or have no funds or ability to do something, we are not very happy? Why do we enjoy deep sleep? Why do we like to be thought well of? Why do we not accept or welcome criticisms?

The second question is: 'Who is Allah?' Who is the Creator of it all? Where is He? What is the meaning of His justice or His compassion or His love for everything He has created?

The third key issue is death: What is it and why do we all fear it? Why are we apprehensive about it? And yet the Prophet tells us, 'Death is nothing other than a long sleep.' It is a natural conclusion to our way of life and yet we do not know its nature. We do not know the experience of leaving the body nor where we go. When we move to a new city, the first thing we find out is how big it is, how to get around, where are the civic amenities, the restaurants and other such information. We hardly ask these questions about the next life, although it is the only thing we really all have in common and which is inevitable.

Then there are the three key shocks in our lives. One of them is the shock of being born. A fetus, which is completely contained in an aqueous, harmonious environment, is suddenly ejected into this world of sounds, sight and senses. The fetus has no need for any of the usual five senses in the womb, but once in the world, they matter very much. If we have weak eyes we spend a great deal of time, effort and money to improve our sight.

The next shock is that of the experience of death. It is a major shock. That is why often there is some preparation for it – we get ill, weak and the people around us get used to it and adjust to the idea of letting us die. The sadness they feel is usually for their own sake because they will miss us.

The third major shock is resurrection. We all believe in that this life is only an intermediate stage for another life. We have come from the darkness of the womb to the darkness of this world and we move in to the unknown of the next world. So what is the nature of resurrection? In the *Qur'ān* we have the most beautiful description by Prophet 'Isa (Jesus) (*may peace be upon him*) when he says:

> ☼ 'And peace on me on the day I was born, and on the day I die, and on the day I am raised to life.' [19:33]

Meaning; 'There is only glory and peace upon me from the moment I was born,' because he was born from an immaculate conception and there is only peace and goodness upon him when he died. And there is only goodness and peace and wellness upon him when he is resurrected. We all go through these phases, even a great prophet.

So essentially this life is a preparation for another phase and that phase has its rules, the same way as when in the womb it has its rules – what the mother eats, how she behaves, her thoughts, conduct and the environment and, of course, the genetic background affects the child. This world has its rules: there is cause and effect, appropriateness, dealing with issues, interacting and relationships, until we grow physically, psychologically, biologically, emotionally and spiritually. Similarly and equally, the next phase also has its rules.

I have selected a few of our teachings from the *Qur'ān* and from the prophetic traditions as to the nature of death and how it comes. The Prophet tells us that the first step of the next life is death. It is like this life too: it has grace and movement and is the last stage of this life and it is the first stage of the next life.

The *Qur'ān* exhorts us to frequently remember death, as does the Prophet and all the enlightened masters of our path. Indeed it is deemed a sign of intelligence to contemplate it, for it is an inevitability. We are told to '*remember death a lot*,' so that we do not pursue frivolous pleasures at the cost of holding ourselves to account. It is not for us to be miserable. It is for us to be joyful, to do things in this life that give us ongoingness and lasting joy and bliss, rather than a few moments of heedless waywardness and frivolous pleasure, for which we pay the price for months and years. Whatever is good we want to endure. Whatever is bad we do not want at all. So we are already practicing longevity or ongoing-*ness*, or forever-*ness*, because this life is subject to time and space which are limited. We cannot have infinite power or boundless knowledge. These things belong to another zone, which is after death.

The Prophet also says: '*This life is like a bridge to the gardens for those who are living their faith, and it is a bridge to hell for those who have no faith, or those who are not prepared to face their Lord*'. And he also says: *'Death is like a long sleep. Its duration is until the day of reckoning.'*

Five times a day we recite our prayer from the *Qur'ān*, praising Allah and acknowledging that it is He who owns and controls the day of reckoning. It does not mean that He does not control today also, but He is subtle and is behind the veils of creation. On the day of reckoning there are no veils anymore.

The *Qur'ān* also says: *'And what do you know of the Day of Judgment?'* [82:17]

And describes it thus: *'The day on which no soul shall control anything for (another) soul; and the command on that day shall be entirely Allah's.'* [82:19]

The Prophet teaches us that *'In this world people act without knowledge. In the next world they have knowledge but they cannot act.'* So we are powerless. Therefore, preparation for the next phase is the action of an intelligent being. We all know we will leave. Are we ready to leave joyfully or shivering with fear and anxiety?

When they asked the Prophet: *'What good is there for somebody who leaves this world?'* If you had a son or a family who pray for you fondly, who remember you well – or as he says, if you have left a *sadaqatun jārriyah*, i.e. a charitable act that continues to benefit others – these things help the soul of the departed.

The soul is that entity in us that carries on forever. Once it comes to this life it takes on the personality of the actual individual. Therefore the fewer imprints there are of me (i.e. my worldly self) upon my soul, the more my soul leads me to the soul-maker, to the divine spirit, to Allah. The purpose of this life, then, is to improve my character, my conduct, and my accountability, so that my heart, which houses the soul, is healthy and alive. If that is the case then I am ready to leave this world at any time, for my accounts are rendered as best as I could. I have seen the perfections behind everything in this existence even though it may appear imperfect. I have seen, therefore, flashes of the qualities and the attributes of Allah. Thus I am ready to face Allah. I am already in tune with His might, with His power, His glory, His majesty, and with His forgiveness.

In terms of mercy (*rahmah*), the Prophet says: *'There are a hundred doors of Rahmah.'* All we have in this creation is one of them – the mercy the mother has for her kids, the mercy you may have for other people who are less endowed than you, the compassion you have in your heart for others, the mercy you have for the injured, dying, destitute or hungry. All of these are according to the prophetic teachings under one umbrella of mercy. He also says: *'99 other doors of mercy are reserved for the Day of Reckoning.'*

After we leave this world the family and others prepare the *Janāzah*, they prepare the dead, pray over him, he is washed and put into the shroud and hopefully they put him down under six feet of dust. And after that they leave. What is our state after we die during the long waiting period before the end of the world? It is here where the prophetic teachings and the *Qur'ān* gives us a lot of wonderful insights. For example, the *Qur'ān* says: *'...and behind them is a barrier until the Day they are resurrected.'* [23:100]

This period after death until resurrection is an interspace or no man's land. It is the name for the place between two countries, that 'no-man's land' – in Arabic *barzakh*. It is neither this nor that, neither of this world where you can act nor of the next world, where everyone is rendering their accounts in the sense of re-living what they have done in this world.

The *ayat* (verses) in the *Qur'ān* and the prophetic teachings tell us that when we leave this world our ongoing condition will be as good as our inner state. If our hearts are tranquil and joyful, full of life and knowledge, knowing we have done our best accountably, responsibly, then our grave is the beginning of the Garden. But it is the reverse if we have only caused trouble, discord and unhappiness to everything around us and have lived totally selfishly; then our graves are a patch of the fire. The *barzakh* implies our inner state, which we take with us. We cannot take our wealth, our relationships, our qualifications, our identities. We are only what we have in our hearts in terms of knowledge of our Creator. Therefore the doors of the heavens open for those of us who have trust and faith in our Creator, who has made this world, the world of physicality and manifestations, which is tiny in relation to the world of the unseen.

The *Qur'ān* reminds us in Surat al-Baqarah that, *'This is the book, there is no doubt in it, a guide to those who are cautiously aware.'* [2:2] There being no doubt in it means that everything in existence is according to perfect ways and the book of the perfect Creator applies to it. It is not haphazard, it is not chaos: it is cosmos. In this book if you read the intention behind Allah's action you will be guided. The key is being among the *muttaqīn*, those who 'guard against evil', who are cautiously aware of falling into wrongful ways.

☼   'Who believe in the unseen, establish prayer, and spend out of what We have provided for them.' [2:3]

Meaning that it is about those who have trust and faith in the unseen and perform their duties in this world and spend from what they possess, whatever it may be – provisions, goodness, knowledge, they give and share with others.

It is a question of trust and faith in the unseen, living in this world while being accountable and at the same time knowing that this world is only a tiny little aspect of the infinite unseen. The two go together. Allah, therefore, instructs the Messenger to give good news to those who have trust and faith that the next world will be better; there will not be injustices, abusiveness and all the lies and deceit we commit in this world, because in the next world we cannot hide anything. The next life will be inverse to this world. Our intentions will manifest more than our physicality. When we meet in the next world we will know each other according to the *rūh*, not so much according to the body, i.e. it is the reverse of what we see now.

In this realm we may see a physical person, but we do not know for sure what is in his heart. The time will come when we are so close together that we know our hearts simply reflect each other and are devoid of anything except the *nur* of Allah, which is called *rūh* – our soul. Therefore the more we progress in perfecting our worship, in knowing that in this world we are simply being exposed to the next world, then we are close together. When we are closer and closer there is less discord between us.

Then Allah promises the perfect garden after this life. In this life we try to create gardens. As soon as you make one there is a drought; as soon as you have planted some seedlings, birds come to peck them out; as soon as fruit ripens, the worms attack it. We have to struggle in this world. This world is an interspace of doing our best, relying upon Allah for His infinite *rahmah* and at the same time maintaining inner contentment in our hearts. The secret is *qalbun salīm* (a wholesome heart). We can bring about a situation where our hearts are well and at peace.

So then when the point of death comes, Allah describes it thus:

☼   'And the stupor of death will come in truth; that is what you were trying to escape.' [50:19]

Meaning that the disorientation or drunken state of not knowing where you are, or who you are when the point of death comes, will come to you by truth. It is written for each one of us to come to that point where we will be completely disorientated. And He says that this is what everyone avoids because we do not know this state and therefore fear it.

We do not know what the nature of death is and what happens in the grave. We need to know more about the agony of the grave and the questionings in the grave. Is everybody questioned? What goes on there? The first few days no doubt one is disorientated because here we are used to living in time and space and when we are placed in the grave time and space no longer apply. We have suddenly been dislodged from these dimensions where we are hanging on to our body. That is why spending the first few nights remembering the dead, praying for them, and reading the *Qur'ān* for them, is important. The soul, the *rūh*, still visits the body, hovering around. It does not know what happened.

Although there is no 'time' in the next phase, there is an echo of this world. Here in our rich heritage and tradition we have a whole chronology of these things, couched in language that we need to decipher because we are living in an age mainly of reason. The prophetic language was mostly applied to people who had faith and trust and who could almost speak with the angels. Nowadays if somebody claims he saw an angel, we'd send them to a psychiatrist. Our times have changed, but the truth has not changed. That is why we need to read within what the prophetic teachings were and take from them what is appropriate for our present mental state.

The Prophet said that those who have done well in this world and have gone with ease will visit their family when they will, and that they will only see good situations. They will be barred from seeing what will hurt them. And the reverse comes to those who have not been prepared for the *ākhirah* (next life). Then there is also the question of whether you feel constriction or expansion in the grave or not. As mentioned earlier, the prophetic teaching is that: *'This world is (like) a prison of those who have faith, trust and knowledge,'* because they know this is restrictive. We naturally want boundless bounty and boundless goodness. The reverse is true of him who has no faith and no trust in Allah: this world is like their palace and the next world is like their prison. If we dwell upon and reflect upon these situations, we will concentrate more on preparing ourselves for departure. If we are ready to depart than we are qualified to arrive.

In the *Qur'ān*, most of the *ayat* about the next life are to do with *yawm al-qiyāmah*, not about the *barzakh*. There are not many descriptions of this intermediate period or interspace. This we get from the prophetic teachings and those who came after him who had also received that knowledge. But in the *Qur'ān* the majority of verses are to do with the Day of Reckoning.

☼   *'O certainly! I swear by the Day of Resurrection.'* [75:1]

Allah also says:

☼   *'...And surely a day with your Lord is like a thousand years of what you count.'* [22:47]

In Arabic the word for day (*yawm*) also means period of time – as Allah describes to us in the *Qur'ān* that as far as your Lord is concerned a day is like a thousand years in our understanding. The Prophet tells us that on the Day of Reckoning there are 50 stations and every step of that day is like a thousand years by our reckoning, implying that time after death is not experienced the same way as time we experience now. It will seem very long or instantaneous. It will be quite different from the time spans we are accustomed to here, like days, weeks, months and so on.

Then on that Day of Reckoning the *Qur'ān* tells us in a variety of verses that we will live as who we really are, not as we pretend or try to be. We are all struggling in this life to try to be good people, good citizens, helpful, following the *dīn*, being transformed by living this path, improving our character, being accountable to each other, loving those who have faith and trust and turning away from those who are corrupt and only living a life of misery.

☼   'That Day, We will seal over their mouths, and their hands will speak to Us, and their feet will testify about what they used to earn' [36:65]

With modern medical diagnostics one cell can tell the whole history and the quality of the organs of the body. One drop of blood can be analyzed to show what is going wrong or what is out of balance in the entire being. Here Allah says that on that day our tongues will bear witness upon us and so will our hands and feet. Where did we go? Why did we run after this and that? What was our intention? We can only do our best and have high expectations of our Creator. We must not think that our actions will save us – the prophetic teachings are full of that. It does not mean we must not do *'amal sālih* (good action). We do, but we must never imagine that it is our good actions that will save us. It is Allah Who will save us. It is Allah's *rahmah* which will save us. Our good action will take us away from wrong action, because we could be doing something worse. We must rely on the Creator of action because Allah has created us <u>and</u> our action. It is His grace that made us do good, His *rahmah* that makes us realize what is good and what is not. It is Allah and being in the proximity of the Creator that we seek.

When Abu Bakr (r.a.) was departing he said, '3 things I have loved in this world: when I had no wealth, when I was ill and when I am dying.' He was asked 'How is that?' He said 'As for wealth, I can only rely upon the maker of wealth; as for illness, I am humbled and I am only looking at Allah's *rahmah* and mercy upon me; and when I leave this world, I am only with my Lord.' The implication being that there is no interference between him and his Lord. So these are the energies that we as *mu'mins* and Muslims are thrilled by, in readiness for the eternal joy.

Allah says in a *Hadith Qudsi*: *'I created you for permanent bliss, not short lived'*. Short-lived goodness is a small indicator of what we love, desire and aspire to, which is ongoingness – the permanent condition of the Garden. And then Allah reminds us in the *Qur'ān*:

☼ 'This is what you were promised, (it is) for everyone who turns frequently (to Allah), keeps (His limits); Who fears the Beneficent Allah in the unseen and comes with a heart returning (in repentance)....' [50:32-33]

Meaning that gardens, joy and eternal bliss are for those who have been responsible and conscious of their Creator without even having met their Creator – simply *bi'l-ghayb* (unseen). *Wa jā'a bi qalbin munīb* – and has come with a 'heart returning', that is, towards Allah.

If we think our salvation lies in action we find it will disappoint us. We like to maintain good relationships with people; yet invariably they will disappoint us, even those who are closest to us. But make an appointment with Allah and carry on! We should not denounce anything but our own fantasy that if we invested in something it should work. Who says it will work? It may become a *favor* upon us. What we aimed to invest in a worldly sense, even with good intentions, may become a chain around us. Say *Bismillah* and, if Allah has taken it away from us, expect better.

Allah tells us in the *Qur'ān* that if we have lost something, something better will come to us, but that result is according to our faith in and high expectations of Allah, according to our *husnu'dh-dhan* (good opinion). We should make that our priority and then deal with human beings because they are all on the same path, wanting to know what is going to be pleasing to Allah and wanting to avoid that which is displeasing to Allah. We want the best for ourselves because we all love the self, because in turn we love the *rūh*, which is *min amri rabbi* (by the command of Allah). It is a capsule of light containing all of Allah's qualities and attributes.

Then Allah says: '(*Their greeting will be*): "*Enter ye here in peace and security.*"' [15:46] In this life we try clumsily to preserve goodness. If anything is good, we try to keep it that way forever. It will not be.

Yet we have to continue that struggle, expecting that ultimately what we are doing will lead us to Him Who is the source of all known and unknown actions and inactions – Allah *subhanahu wa ta'ala.*

'He made the Hereafter an abode to reward His believers because this world cannot contain what He wishes to bestow upon them.'

15: THE MERCY AND BLESSINGS OF ILLNESS

There can be no goodness without the seed of what is considered bad within it. Death is one day closer after birth. It is a great gift to see an aspect of goodness or ease within a difficulty.

Every event or experience can be viewed from different perspectives and thus interpreted differently. A loss or difficulty can be perceived as an opportunity for renewal or a calamity. The true believer who trusts in the permanent and constant generosity and mercy of Allah will regard illness and disease as an opportunity and develop greater sensitivity and awareness regarding matters of health, diet and responsibility.

The *mu'min* (believer), the *muttaqi* (he who is cautiously aware of everything he does), always seeks for the meaning behind the event. He or she wonders what Allah is passing on to them because they know He loves them. The *mu'min* knows we have been created in order to know our Lord. Through the *Qur'ān* and his *sacred hadith* (*hadith qudsi*) Allah tells us that He has only created us in order to be known and to worship Him. So the *muttaqi* is living inwardly with ecstasy in the knowledge that Allah is *Rabbu'n-rahim, Rabbu'n-ra'uf, Rabbu'n- wadūd, Rabbu'n-latif* (a Merciful Lord, a Most Affectionate Lord, an All- Loving Lord, a Subtle Lord).

When any event or process befalls us, the attuned Muslim will always try to read the signs: should he now be quiet? Is it time to open up other doors? What is the message behind the event? And this applies in expansion and contraction. Whenever we are afflicted with *dis*-ease, we not only try to find treatment for the symptoms, but also the cause, because deep down our nature is programmed to want ease and harmony. *Dis*-ease is something we do not like. If you are steadfast and patient during illness, you will see wonderment and gifts that are not normally given to us during times of ease. During the time of ease, fullness and increased provision, we just run around more in the outer and therefore make more mistakes.

It is always during times of restriction that the inner grows. When the inner grows, it balances the outer. Then outer wealth or outer power will not overwhelm us, nor tarnish our heart, nor bring in all the *shaytanic* elements. That is why we need to be in constant balance between illness and wellness, between breathing in and breathing out.

Most illnesses also, especially the chronic ones and those which we have acquired over a period of time have messages in them. I have, in my lifetime, known so many people who have become hard of hearing partly because they have spent years avoiding hearing a nagging wife, partner or boss. It is the same with sight. I have also observed that generally people who are long-sighted are wiser or have a propensity of metaphorical far-sightedness. Equally short-sightedness is also because of a deeper desire not to see or recognize something – the stress of studying or excessive amounts of fine print we have to read to sort out our bank balance! Some people have high blood pressure because their normal energies are not expressed in a physical or outer way and they bottle it up.

Certainly anything to do with the heart is the same. A heart can be hardened in more ways than just with atherosclerosis. Apart from dietary and genetic influences, a heart can seize up if the head is over-used and balance is lost. The head is to do with reasoning: deciding whether it is the right time or place to act. Is it the right season for us to put the seed in the ground? Is it a time for expansion or is it a time to accept contraction? We cannot have either without its opposite to balance it.

Outer expansion always needs to be balanced by inner expansion. Otherwise, like an overloaded boat, we will sink. These are the laws and the ways of Allah in the *Qur'ān* and in the way of the Prophet himself, for he was known as the 'walking *Qur'ān*'. We eulogize him and celebrate his life, but how many of our homes would he visit if he came back to this world? If his *rūh* (soul) were passing through would he come and visit us? Are we ready to be hugged by the Prophet? Are we ready to follow unconditionally? Do we love the *Qur'ān* in the sense that we are living it or is it only to be read when somebody dies or is getting married or divorced? We have, as Muslims, got this incredible gift of the *Qur'ān*, but how many of us are truly assimilating it and following its map? That is why we are hardly getting to the destination. We assume and presume we are Muslims, but we are Muslim in name only. Are we transformed by our *dīn* (way of life)? Allah describes the human condition perfectly in the *Qur'ān*:

> ☼ 'Surely man is created of a hasty temperament, Being greatly grieved when evil afflicts him, And niggardly when good befalls him, Except those who pray, Those who are constant in their prayer, And those in whose wealth there is a fixed portion.' [70:19-24]

The foundation of *salāt* (prayers) is *sajdah* (prostration), the practice of disappearance of the self, so that we recognize 'we' do not exist. Our existence is by the mercy of Allah to recognize His presence. *Sajdah* means being without any thought and any illusion. In that state we are gone. Where? To Him who has brought us, Who is here after all of us have gone – only His *Nūr* (light) will remain.

As for those of us who are perpetually in a state of awareness, we are responsible for whatever Allah has given to us of value. Wealth (*māl*) is everything you incline towards. The root verb is *māla/yamīlu*: to lean towards. We call it 'wealth' because everyone is inclined towards wealth. And if we cannot get it, we are inclined towards the wealthy and give them much greater respect. That is why when *Mullah Nasruddin* came in his dirty clothes to a reception they showed him out. He went to put on fine robes and when he returned, they brought him to the high-table. So he sat there shoving the food into his sleeves. Everyone was shocked. 'What are you doing?' they asked. He replied: 'Clearly you didn't invite me. You invited my clothes. So it is the clothes that must eat!'

Indeed we are impressed with the wealthy. That is why we dress up nicely and put on our suits when we want to go to the bank. We do not realize that they are the hunters and we are the hunted because they have the power and we are disempowered – yet we love to be empowered. Who has power? Every week a despot or tycoon tumbles down. A year ago tycoon chief executive officers were regarded like demi-gods. Now they have all fallen in stature, like the statue of Lenin.

What remains is the divine ways, the divine maps, the divine laws, and the divine patterns – the journey to know the permanent and deal with the impermanent. Let Allah deal with us, and then we can deal with the opposites, with the sickness and the wellness, and the ups and downs. If our hearts are not centered in balance, then we too are one day up, one day down. As we yo-yo up and down every half an hour, our family has to guess when we are in a good mood so that they can come and talk to us. Otherwise, the message goes out, *'Daddy is in a bad mood again!'* Catch the mode and the mood will be all right. If we don't catch the mode, then the mood will ruin us.

We are essentially an eternal battery or light called the *rūh* (soul), which is activated by the self (*nafs*). The self has in it aspects of hereditary biology and a lot to do with upbringing and the environment. The soul is eternal, perfect light. The two go together. That light has a lamp on it with a certain coloration called the self

– or personality. If that color is pure and simple, then we are pure and simple – from Allah, to Allah, by Allah – and our time here as a prelude to the eternal Garden will be wonderful. If we are not, then we are in trouble. One minute may be hell, another the garden.

Our disorientation arises from not being to tune to that which is the highest in us, which is beyond duality, beyond mental discrimination. Therefore, we accept the zone of this consciousness of causality – this is good, this is bad, this is right and that is fine. But then we also move out of that state. Our fasting is part and parcel of that movement towards the higher. I'tikāf (retreat or seclusion) means emptying out. You empty the body, you empty the mind, and thereby you empty the heart. Free of obscuration, the lamp shines from the light within and you are a then full human being. This is the gift of our dīn. Allah reminds us:

> ☼ 'And it may be that you dislike a thing which is good for you and you like a thing which is bad for you.' [2:216]

Why impose restrictions on ourselves, like i'itikaf? So that you have expansion and Allah reminds us:

> ☼ 'And for him who fears the standing before his Lord, there will be two gardens (i.e. in Paradise).' [55:46]

Of the two gardens, one is here in our hearts: a garden of joy in the knowledge that we have nothing of our own, that we are only living by Allah's rahmah, for Allah's acceptance. We only have the one heart. If we realize this, we can experience the inner garden at any time. If we lose our balance by excessive reliance on rationalism, we may experience trouble. But we deal with it 'Bismi'llah' (in the name of Allah) and then it's no longer attached to our emotions. If we do our best and leave the rest to Allah, the result will be beyond our expectations, but not necessarily according to the way we have plotted. If we do our best and we suddenly find a door closes to humble us, to keep us in our position of conscious dependence on Allah, we find the result is better than we thought it would be. These are the ways that the *mu'min* (believer) connects the seen with the unseen.

Take solace and security in the unseen. We know that the seen and the unseen meet and we are the interspace between these two zones. And we know that tasting the garden here is a prelude to the eternal Garden. Avoiding the fires of agitation, greed and anxiety here is also avoiding the Fire after we leave this world. This world is a crucible, a laboratory if you will, for us to know that Allah's patterns and desires are perfect and this implies knowledge and action. These are married together, for there can never be knowledge without action or action without knowledge.

Allah says: *'And by your actions I will increase your* īmān *(faith).'*

So that we become living entities fully present in the moment – not half of us buried in the misery of the past and the other half immersed in the insecurity of the future. We should maintain our *wudu'*. That is why the Prophet says: *'Your* ṣalāt *will give you nourishment if you have presence of heart.'* For that reason though our ablution we seal ourselves from the world, declaring Allah is greater than we can ever imagine, submitting to Him, entering into that mode and going into our *sajdah* (prostration) as though we were never here before. And when we sit back: *'Astaghfiru'llah* (I ask Allah forgiveness/cover): and then glorification: *'subhānallah* (Glory be to Allah). Allah has given us this apparent power of being independent or separate so that we can sit and invoke the truth that we know that Allah is both the seen and the unseen. Finally we become as Allah describes: *'Those who remain constant in their* ṣalāt *(prayers),'* perpetually in that state of connectivity.

'Your remedy is within you – but you do not sense it. Your sickness is within you – but you do not perceive it.'
– Imam 'Ali

16: PROPHETIC LEADERSHIP

Understanding the impact of context is vital. Not only was the Prophet Allah's Messenger, but he was also a leader in his own times.

The exact date of birth of our blessed Prophet (S) was not properly recorded and there are a few differences of opinion in determining the exact date. Generally it is agreed he was born in 570 CE, on either the 12th or 17th of the month called *Rabi' ul-Awwal.* As lovers of our *dīn* (way of life) and our Prophet, we should want to celebrate that event all the time. During that month, some people celebrate it for two or three weeks. Any remembrance of the event of the great advent of the seal of the prophets is a good remembrance.

What is the meaning of 'prophetic leadership'? It is very important to go to the Arabic origin of the meaning of the words *nabiy* and *rasūl. Nabiy* is prophet. *Rasūl* is apostle or messenger. Not every *nabiy* is a *rasul,* but every *rasul* is a *nabiy.* The root of *nabiy* is from *naba'a,* which is to inform, notify, announce, make known, or to advise. These are the relevant meanings of *naba'a.* In modern Arabic broadcasting stations are also called the *anbā'* services. In other words, the prophet is he who broadcasts the good news and the warning, and makes known the Light of the Creator. He also makes known the map and the way of creation and notifies them of the message. Prophecy and prediction are also related to the same root – and ultimately prophecy is that everything will come to an end, except that which is within you. Prediction is that no matter what situation gives you pleasure, it will also give you displeasure.

The prophecy is that we all are looking for an inner state that gives us long, durable contentment. That is the ultimate news. Every one of us is looking for happiness. That quest implies that there is already a zone or a reference point within you that is reliably there to give you inner joy. That is the good news. And the warning is that if you do not adhere to the appropriate barriers, boundaries and skills of the correct courtesies – whether it is to do with your body, your mind or your heart – you will not attain that constancy within you.

That is the good news. The word *rasūl* is an envoy, apostle and emissary, from *rasala*, to send, delegate. Other meanings from the same word have connotations of ease of flow: *irsāl* for example means ease and length of flow. A *risālah* is a message or treatise. But what is relevant to us is the implicit idea of a delegate or envoy delivering something special. Our glorious Prophet Muhammad was both a *nabiy* and a *rasūl*. We have been told that there were thousands upon thousands of *anbiyā'* (prophets), but fewer *rusul*, or apostles. In our heritage of *Islam* we have the great advantage of acknowledging so many of the great *rusul* who were also *anbiyā'*, especially those known as *Ulu'l-'Azm*, the great five, especially of the *Ibrahimi* (Abrahamic) tradition. Thus we have a very rich and valuable tradition if we absorb it and live by it.

There are a few verses from the *Qur'ān* which introduce these terms, *nabiy* or *nabā'* or *nubuwwah*, as well as *risālah*. At the beginning of the last 30th section or *juz'* of the *Qur'ān* Allah says:

> ☼ 'Of what do they ask (one another)? About the great news, About which they are in disagreement.' [78:1-3]

The great news is ultimately to do with the end of the journey. What happens after death? What is next life? What is the nature of the next life? How can we be prepared if we believe in the hereafter – the *ākhirah*? What can we do now to be prepared so that it will be a happy ending and a happy beginning after we leave this world? How can we be prepared for eternal life, because it is no longer subject to time and space? Every moment there will be a change because of this constant movement that occurs within this existence. Anything you have, whether in your mind, in your hands, in your pocket or in your body, will change. But after death we move into a new zone that is no longer subject to change. How can we be prepared for that eventuality?

☼   Allah says: 'Certainly everyone shall come to know; nay certainly they shall soon come to know.' [78:4-5]

Every self will experience this departure from the body. The implication is that you and I are not what we think we are. We are essentially a *rūh* that has come to activate a self, which has identified with the body. That is why a three-year-old child says: 'I', a thirty-year- old man also says: 'I', and a sixty-year old will also say: 'I'. So there is constancy in this 'I', which proves that it contains an element which is permanently reliable and ongoing, which is the *rūh*. It is like a self- charging battery, but that *rūh* is connected with an individual identity. Every one of us is different in our *self*, which is called the *nafs*.

So we have the *rūh* plus the *nafs* and this journey is constantly in change until we leave this world. Then, just as the *nafs* has been groomed or trained to experience reality, so will the experience of the next world be shaped. If the *nafs* has completely yielded to the *rūh*, then it is *rūh*. That is why the *Qur'ān* uses the word *rūh* for *nafs* interchangeably. The purpose is for this dispersion to acknowledge the gatheredness and then be united with it. Thus the purpose of our journey in this life and the teachings of the Prophet and the leadership of the prophetic character and qualities is all in order for the *nafs* to be subdued or to give up that pretence that it has any independent power and for it to yield to the *rūh* in it, to yield to

Allah, and to be obedient and groomed. That is the whole purpose of all of paths and religions.

We have the good fortune to have a very clear *dīn* – a very clear path – a pattern of conduct which you can implement and apply wherever you are and whoever you are. That is why it says in the *Qur'ān*: 'And We have not sent you but as a mercy to all creation,' [21:107] so that there is no confusion and no arguments about the way to abandon the lower tendencies in us. We all know the lower tendencies within us. We get angry, mean, suspicious, frightened and insecure. All of these lower tendencies are natural. The natural way is to rise above them is to realize them and then realize Allah's perfection of wealth, security, power and everlastingness and then let those higher qualities, which we can understand, cover the lower qualities in us, which we experience. It is a displacement process: moving from the lower to the higher, which is already there.

☼   Allah also tells us about prophets: 'And thus did We make for every prophet an enemy, the Shaytans from among men and jinn, some of them suggesting to others varnished falsehood to deceive (them), and had your Lord pleased they would not have done it, therefore leave them and that which they forge.' [6:112]

Wherever there is light there is darkness. Wherever there is goodness there is also evil. The meal that will give you strength and nourishment can give you sickness – if you eat of it in excess, if you abuse it or if it has not been preserved well. So it is the relevance of this situation that matters. The prophets and the great *'awliyā'* (saints) and messengers have often had the worst people close to them. It is in the nature of existence that context and application matters.

If the prophet or messenger wanted to be saved from all the outer troubles, he would also have remained in isolation. Now isolation is important and helpful, whether it is *i'ikāf,* or whether it is *khalwa* (solitary retreat), so that you withdraw from outer distractions and begin to read the 'book' within you. At the moment we study the *Qur'ān* outwardly until we realize it is absolutely true, or until we realize that this truth is also in our *fitrah* – primal patterns inscribed within us. Allah's patterns are everywhere.

Another verse: *'Certainly, a Messenger has come to you from among yourselves; grievous to him is your falling into distress, excessively solicitous respecting you; to the believers (he is) compassionate,'* [9:128]. The Prophet is not an angel that sometimes appears and sometimes disappears. He is a normal human being who ate, slept, had a family, had wives, endured trouble, battles and concerns, so that the outer conduct is familiar and we are not surprised.

> ☼   'And We did not send any messenger but with the language of his people, so that he might explain to them clearly; then Allah makes whom He pleases err and He guides whom He pleases and He is the Mighty, the Wise.' [14:4]

Every people had received a messenger to speak to them according to their understanding, in their language and according to their culture so that they would have no excuse that they had not heard the true revealed knowledge of Allah. If anything is of a different culture or language we need to make a bridge in order to understand it. In this case it was a prophet who came to a people and spoke a language that was a very important language of the day because it is related to Hebrew and to other ancient languages, and also because that language has been preserved so its meaning is still intelligible to us.

'Bi lisāni qawmī' (the tongue of my people) implies that when you and I try and talk to our children we must speak their language. It is no use speaking to them of erudite things about the higher elements within the heart. You have to speak a child's language.

Likewise you have to speak the language of the people according to who they are. The prophetic quality and character was centered on that. His advice was: *'Speak to the people according to what they understand.'* Otherwise, you will either be elevating yourself, making yourself something special, or causing misunderstanding.

Then Allah describes our glorious Prophet: *'And most surely you conform (yourself) to sublime morality'* [68:4]. And then Allah also tells us in the *Qur'ān*: *'Certainly you have in the Messenger of Allah an excellent exemplar for him who hopes in Allah and the latter day and remembers Allah much.'* [33:21]

What this means is that we as human beings need to be led out of our inner personal as well as community confusion. If you do not lead yourself personally, care for your character and elevate yourself to that which is possible within you, then a community of high character will not come about. It will be an inferior community. Charity starts at home. Every one of us, therefore – if we truly love Allah and His creation and acknowledge His generosity – should also love the higher in us and despise that which is low in us. It is very common in so many circles nowadays to talk about self-love or loving yourself. But how can you love the mean part of you? How can you love that part of you that is suspicious or that suddenly flies off the handle and becomes angry in the wrong place? We cannot love the lower qualities in us. We can love the higher qualities, which are potentially in us. But then we need to replace the lower qualities with the higher qualities, which ultimately reflect the perfections of Allah.

This is the process and this is true leadership. And our glorious Prophet showed us by his character and conduct how this is the only purpose of creation: to live as though you are leaving this world any minute and to live as though everybody else is the same as you. And as Allah says: *'...He between whom and you was enmity would be as if he were a warm friend'* [41:34]. This means that potentially that gangster, if he is reformed, can become a man of Allah. He can become free from all of the fantasy in his mind, or other imprisonments, so that he is free from anything other than being enslaved to Allah.

Leadership implies guiding us, setting an example for us and conducting us. In our case we Muslims were even more fortunate in that he became, by choice of people and by acknowledgement of people, the *amir* or the leader of the people in every way, existentially and otherwise. Life was not separated, for example, into secular, religious or spiritual. That is why our *din* cannot be subdivided. It is a way of life, a way of conduct towards yourself, towards others, towards your creator and towards communities, the environment and so on. That is why we need brothers and sisters of high quality so that we see in them our reflections, so all of us can rise. That is why the Prophet said: *'In my time, there were the best of people'.*

The *Qur'ān* also addresses the believers and followers of the Prophet Muhammad: *'You are the best of the nations raised up for (the benefit of) men; you enjoin what is right and forbid the wrong and believe in Allah.'* [3:110]. It doesn't mean the potential is not there all the time, but that it may be more difficult for it to be expressed because of additional exposure, additional poisons and additional difficulties.

The qualities we see in the Prophet are as follows: the quality of modesty, he was one of the most modest men. He was never haughty or pretentious. Chastity is another quality. He always had that gentle way, as though he was even ashamed. He had steadfastness, patience, self-control, sobriety, self-discipline, mildness, and natural piety. How can piety become a natural thing? It is the state of being aware that any minute we may leave this world. Are we ready? Are we relaxed about it? Do we have a lot of affairs to put in order? Then he had courage. He was the first to go into battle. There were more than seventy battles in Madinah. He had magnanimity and intrepidity, which is the opposite of despair. He always had natural composure and presence. He was not pompous. He had fortitude, the opposite of submissiveness. He had forbearance and self-containment.

He was also manly. He would always rise to the occasion. The opposite of manliness is apathy. He was manly in that he was concerned about the poor and the *miskin* and the widowed women and did something about it. He had natural endurance. He could carry on and on. Then there was wisdom. He was considered to be the most intelligent person and he was able to retain things. Once he heard something, he would retain it forever, starting with the *Qur'ān* and then moving on to other things. And then he was a reasonable and rational man. Everything had its place. He had clarity and understanding – an excellence of understanding. That is why he used to say: *'I have eyes behind me, I can see from behind.'* He did not mean physical eyes. It meant the sensitivity of understanding.

His capacity for learning was immense. And then he was the most just being. That is why, even in his youth, people trusted him. He was friendly and people could approach him. He always had inner harmony. That is why people loved to be close to him to pick up that energy. He had concern for his family, for his relatives, for the tribe and for mankind altogether. He always taught, lived and interacted with fair play and was not excessive. That is why in Islam monopoly and similar things are not allowed. With regard to honest dealings, he was the most honest person in that he would point out any iniquities or excess in any transaction. He had amicability and piety in that he was constant in wanting to do good to everyone. This is the ultimate meaning of piety. These were the qualities of the real leader. If you compare those qualities with those of our leaders nowadays, you will see why we are in such a mess. The last thing a real leader wants to do is to advertise himself. Nowadays, in so-called modern politics, you can never move an inch without advertising yourself. It is exactly the opposite of the prophetic way.

Furthermore, we should bear in mind that historically at the time of *Islam,* or the advent of the *Muhammadi Islam,* there were two types of leadership. One was the Greek-style leadership, which was based on democracy in a real sense; that is, special people who were considered to be citizens (they were the minority in their land) would elect one amongst them and he would be the same as them. The best example yet is Alexander the Great. He was the ultimate conqueror of the world and anybody who came to him would just call him 'Alexander '. He was never, 'Your Excellency, Your Highness,' or fifty other titles. He was elected by the citizens who were the free men in the cities – for the political unit was the city-state. The other model of rulership was that of the great Persian Empire that conquered Greece by sea. Kingship in Persia was considered to be by divine right. Alexander the Great was most curious as to what this form of rule was because it begged the question: What is divine right? This notion echoed the idea of a prophet leading his people. The Kings of Persia were sometimes great and at other times corrupt. They were great when the spiritual element was very high and that is why the ultimate example for humanity was the prophetic model of leadership, which is that he who knows Allah best is the most desired leader of the people. That, in essence, is the model of our *dīn*: he leads who knows the perfect light and Allah's qualities and ways, meaning he who best knows his *dīn*, his *Qur'ān* and the way of the prophet (*Sunnah*) and lives it, not merely talking about it – after all, the prophetic teaching also warns us: *'The greatest evil that will come amongst the so-called 'ulama' is the love to lead.'* This is the warning. The Prophet teaches us that the love of being honored and the love of remembrance of Allah do not meet in one heart.

Another Prophetic teaching relevant to leadership is: *'Do not be taken by him who has power;'* for example, a sultan with worldly power. The allegory of riding a lion is appropriate: Whoever sees someone riding on a lion thinks they would like that power for themselves, but they do not know what that man's own condition is. The fellow who is riding the lion knows that if he falls, the lion is going to eat him.

For four hundred years in Iraq, we had so many *walis* (governors) appointed by Istanbul. Because they had had to pay a fee before they were appointed a *wali*, they had to make up the loss to their own pocketbook quickly. Hence there was a lot of corruption.

Here is a story that highlights this historical reality: a man died leaving immense wealth to his son. He had told him where it was buried (many kilos of gold and jewels) and that he must only give it to the most wretched person on this earth. The son had asked his father what he meant by the most wretched person. His father said: 'Whoever desperately needs this'. The son spent several years travelling, looking for such a person. He saw that everybody wanted money. Everybody wanted wealth to build more houses, buy more camels and so on. He realized, however, that they were not wretched but just greedy idiots. So he went back and forth until he saw a new *wali* had been appointed in Baghdad. It was usually the case that the previous *wali* would be deposed and driven out of his office. While the new one was just arriving with pomp and ceremony, he saw the last *wali* being ignominiously dragged through the streets. So he said: *'Now I know who is the most wretched.'* The next morning the Baghdadi people go to pay their respects and to see how they can make money out of him. This young man goes in and says: *'I have a big gift for you. My father left his great fortune and it is for you.'* The new *wali* asked: *'But how come? I don't know your father.'* He replied: *'No, but he knew you. He told me to give it to the most wretched person. You saw what happened to the person before you! Yet here you are!'*

What lies at the heart of the matter is the love of Allah's qualities. We all love power – He is the most powerful. We all love wealth – He has wealth beyond measure. We all love generosity – He is the ultimate in generosity. We love patience – He is patience itself. The truth is that we are totally in love with Allah's qualities. So let us then hate our lower qualities and replace them with Allah's qualities, without pretending that we are now becoming 'closer to God'. Allah says that: *'He is closer to him than his jugular vein'* [50:16]. We do not recognize that because we are not looking at Him, but elsewhere.

So to remember our glorious Prophet is to remember his qualities, to remember his presence, to remember how he was constantly, thinking, living, operating and walking with Allah's light. That is why Ayesha (r.a.) said: *'He was like the walking Qur'ān.'* We collect copies of the *Qur'ān*, but what have we absorbed of it? What has been internalized? Let our remembrance of the prophet be the remembrance of his qualities. Let us yearn for some of those qualities to come to us. Let us be worthy of being His lovers. Let us be worthy of being Muslims. Let us be under the banner of *Islam*.

The prophet is he who gives the good news and the warning, and makes known the Light of the Creator.

17: LIVING ISLAM: SUPPLICATION, ACTION & THE SEVEN FOUNDATIONAL ATTRIBUTES

The path of intelligent submission to truth – Islam – is transformative and leads to self-realization & enlightenment.

We have all emerged from the wonderful month of *Ramadān*. No doubt many of us are still benefiting from the abstention and heightened awareness that comes with the month. I have no doubt many of us are still in a state of correct inner harmony as a result of the month spent in heightened awareness of Allah's presence and also of the constancy of the *shaytanic* tendencies that are in existence everywhere.

If we can maintain that state of *Ramadān* whilst we are more active, then we are more likely to have a year in which we are less afflicted, less affected by material, physical, mental and spiritual disturbance. Allah reminds us in the *Qur'ān*: *'O man! You are struggling towards your Lord toilingly, until you meet Him.'* [84:6]. Allah gives us the news and the truth that turmoil and struggle will continue at all levels.

I would like to share with you aspects of *du'a* (supplication), calling on Allah. What does it mean? How does it work? Why does it not work some of the time? Who is calling whom? What are the secrets of supplication? Allah reminds us that we are struggling all the time – for shelter, protection, food and provision. These are the fundamental, primal, primitive struggles. But when we have enough food and shelter we will begin to question the meaning of life. Why do we want happiness and yet we are not happy all the time? Where is the mercy of Allah, for He says *'My mercy is in every situation'*? We are all created wanting contentment and yet we are not content.

Allah reminds us on numerous occasions in the *Qur'ān* that He has created this life so that we will begin to realize our actions, so that we are challenged all the time. *Balā'* is a challenge. *Balā'* is about learning to give up. The original meaning is to wear out. To be worn out is to be exhausted. Physical exhaustion is often simply a result of a lack of spiritual energy. If we are spiritually energized, then we know that Allah is in charge. Where is our exhaustion coming from? Exhaustion is the heat that comes from the resistance of not being totally in Allah's hand. That is exhaustion. An engine is exhausted and burnt out because it does not yield itself to what it has been designed for or the electrical current that is behind it. The conundrum we face is that in spite of not liking to be exhausted we do get exhausted. So what is the answer? The answer lies within us. We have to first stop that worldly activity which precedes this state of depletion, if it is not right. It is, after all, generating a lot of heat and resistance.

The meaning of Islam is not to resist, to submit to the truth. The truth is that we are going to die. The truth is that time is relative – Allah tells us in the *Qur'ān*: *'A day with Allah is like a thousand years.'* So time is relative. Look back to the last 20 years. What have you done? How much have you worried? How many nights didn't you sleep? How many times have you quarreled? How many times have you shouted, whether it's at the poor person next to you or someone on the telephone? What was it all for? Are you better now? Are you happier now? Have you got the formula? Any intelligent person would want to have woken up to the meaning of it all.

☼   Allah is He: 'Who created death and life that He may try you – which of you is best in deeds; and He is the Mighty, the Forgiving.' [67:2]

The best action is that which does not leave us with expectations that may not be met. The good action is that we will feel good about it for a long period, not for just one instant. Pleasure is when we are tranquil and content for a moment – soon it will also give us displeasure. Joy is that which will last. All human beings are seekers of perpetual happiness and the answer to finding it does not lie outside. It lies inside us. The outside is very easy to tackle. We blame others and become confused and imagine that the next place, the next wife, next house or next country, will bring us happiness. But for how long can we do this? We carry the same rubbish with us because it is inside. It is the software that is not right. We may move on to the next place but the pollution is already there so the same thing repeats itself. And then we blame the politicians and everyone else – others! – all over again.

The right actions are the actions for which we have no expectations of recompense. That is called *fi sabili'llah*. Allah does not *need* us. We need to learn how to avoid being *fi sabil an-nafs* to stop acting for our own self's sake! This does not mean that we should not care for ourselves, for the donkey. Our body is the donkey. Care for it. But are we here entirely to live for that? We have to care for our family, but are we going to be slaves to them for the rest of our lives? We cannot accept that and we will resent it. Care for them, certainly. Care for the immediate so that we care for that which is before the immediate and after the immediate.

All of these are necessary steps, but the ultimate step is that you are *'abd Allah* (servant or slave of Allah). Allah says: *'I am near.'* [2:186]. Allah also tells us in the *Qur'an* that He is closer to us that the jugular vein. Allah is the Ever-Close, so close that we cannot talk about distance. Distance is no longer relevant and yet also subtle: we cannot touch, buy or sell our Creator. So the key issue is to call on Allah. We need to call on Allah. We need to call on Allah's *rahmah*. We need to call upon Allah now.

There are seven attributes of Allah that are the foundation of all the other attributes. Allah's attributes have no end. We are reminded by the Prophet to learn, know and understand ninety-nine of His attributes. If we are truly and utterly tuned to these attributes according to the prophetic teachings, we are on our way to the garden. So it is for that reason we have been created in need. We always will need something from Allah, so that we are humbled, so that by that humbleness we realize his glory. The two must go together. We cannot have one without the other.

Now these seven glorious, fundamental attributes are:

1. Al-Hayy (The Ever-Living). We experience life for a short period. So He allows us exposure to that which is infinite because He has programmed us to have this *hayat* (life) which we want to continue forever. Whenever a time is good we want it to last forever. Many people always yearn for longer life. It is good to have a longer life if we are going to discover the Life-giver. It is a wonderful thing to wish others a longer life, provided they will truly discover the Ever-Present, Allah. Then they are ready to stay or not to stay. Otherwise, what is the point of longer life? It is more consumption, more disasters, more needs, and arguments with the banks and with families.

2. Al-Qādir (The Able). Everything possible, existential and otherwise is in His hand. We also have *qudrah* (ability) but it is limited. I have a bit of *qudrah* to talk or to walk for a while or to help or to read, whereas His *qudrah* is limitless. So He allows us to have exposure to the treasury of the King of kings.

3. Al-Murid (The Willer). *Iradah* is will. In Arabic the word for will is also related to love, or desire. The power of will as it pertains to Allah is in the impetus for commanding or willing things to come into being or as a general decree, and this power is intimately connected with love. *Iradah* and its different levels and layers are given much attention in our traditions. Will ultimately becomes love or *'ishq*, passion for Him who has created passion, who has created us all and the cosmos. There are many, many layers of 'willingness', culminating in *'ishq*, which implies diving into that which you love. This is what the Sufis refer to as *fanā' fi'llah*. If we love the source of all love, then we do not exist anymore. We do not recognize our own separate independent existence. It is the enlightened person who tries to unite his will with Allah's will because we know Allah's will is what will come to pass. Our will, on the other hand, may or may not be made manifest.

4. *Al-'Alim* (The All-Knowing). Allah knows everything; we do not. We know very little, but we pray and do our best to come to know that which we need to know at the time we need to know it. This is where we, as Muslims, have the enormous advantage of a great heritage of *Islam* and the *Qur'ān*, the prophetic teachings and those who came after the Prophet who continued being illumined as *'awliyā'*. The mapping is accessible and clear. But equally, for every advantage there is a disadvantage. Here we have the disadvantage of being given information that is familiar and therefore not immediately usable. So we become impertinent – we say: 'I have heard this' or we say: 'I have heard this *surah* before'. It is as if there is a king who is looking after his people very well, ensuring their health, safety, and security, and you are the head of a family living in that realm, under that king. One day and announce to the household, including a four year old child, that the king is dead. The effect upon that child is almost negligible because he cannot appreciate the fact that this just, good king who was providing all of these services has gone. He is just used to the information and to the services being provided. We are used to the *Qur'ān* in this way, and to the Prophet's teachings and the teachings of others.

If information does not impact upon you for transformation, then it is lost. And that is the case with many structured religions. Many of us as Muslims also fall into that trap. Information is a bundle of energy. It is like the energy that comes into your cell phone. If we do not respond, it is useless. Similarly when we hear *lā ilāha illa'llah* and *Muhammadun Rasūl Allah,* if it does not make us stand upside-down, inside-out, then it has not benefited us. We have not begun to see the one behind the multitude. And the access to that unified sight is *Muhammadun Rasūl Allah* – in other words, invoking his name, his prophethood, links you to how he saw his Creator in every situation.

So the fourth attribute which we share with Allah, is *'ilm* – He knows all. Ultimately, the true, pious, decent, wholesome *mu'min* will come to know that he does not know, but we have certainty that He who knows all will give us what we need to know at the time we need to know it. Then we are inwardly secure. Then we know that we have *rabbun wadūd, rabbun halīm, rabbun karīm, rabbun jabbār, rabbun muhīt.*

5. Al-Samī' (The All-Hearing). We hear by means of organs, our ears, but divine hearing is beyond any means or apparatus. Allah does not need any means to 'hear', for He is the Creator of means. He hears before we have even spoken. It is like Nabiy Ibrahim when he was thrown into the fire. He said: *'It is enough for me not to ask because I know He knows.'*

6. Al-Basīr (The All-Seeing). We need sight. *Basar* is sight. *Mubsira* is the eyes. As we grow, that outer sight slowly is transferred to insight, whereupon it then becomes *basirah* (insight). In the Arabic language even a blind man can be called *basīr* because he can have insight. Allah sees all, again without the need for eyes.

7. Al-Mutakallim (The Communicator or Connector). The entire cosmos is connected by the One. Every existence is like a bead on an infinite *tasbih*. The thread of it is the One. Otherwise there would be no cosmos. The entire cosmos is totally and utterly held in a unified field by the unifier of it all, by the one and only, Allah.

These are the attributes. When we call upon Allah, when we want to know something, we call upon Him as *ya 'Alim, ya 'Alim* (O All- Knowing). What are we doing when we are calling? If we consider ourselves separate as an independent entity, then it will never work. Call upon whatever for a thousand years, it will never work. That is why most people's supplications and calls are never answered. The way they supplicate doesn't work. At least they are kept a little quiet for that time so the family can have a bit of peace.

There are courtesies to every situation. There is a courtesy between us now. We are sitting quietly and these wonderful people have provided a pleasant, quiet place, with reasonable temperature control. Now, the courtesy of this place is to internalize. Courtesy when we walk is to move on – we take care not to bump into everybody else. The courtesy of *du'a* is to put the self aside. The entire exercise of happiness, contentment, joy, getting ready for the garden is to put our self aside because it is the self that causes us all our troubles. With the self we are all in deep trouble, yet paradoxically without the self we cannot exist. With a mind at work we will always experience trouble, but without a sound mind we will be fools.

We have to start with the lower self: pamper it like a child. Then when we grow up we know that the self is like a zoo full of animals. So we contain it. And then we grow connected and concerned with the *nur*, the original light of Allah. We all want light. We are not concerned with shadows anymore. – we have done enough of shadow play. We know that what comes must go. We know that what is going to give us pleasure now will give us displeasure tomorrow. It is the perpetual play of opposites. This is what life is about. But the Life-

Giver and His *nur* illumines these dualities and gives coherence.

So the first condition of supplication is to recognize our weakness, our meekness and the impossibility of being able to do anything. Then we are beginning to know what *tawakkul* is. When you have *tawakkul*, meaning recognizing we have nothing of our own and that all is in Allah's hand, we are truly depending on Allah. Then there is no doubt anymore because 'we' do not exist. He is going to give us what is appropriate – so we are free from our fantasy of 'I want this' and 'I want to do that first'. That is all madness. Sane people in this world are, spiritually speaking, appear mad. We know it is going to come to an end, and therefore our concentration on what is important shifts. We know we are going to die.

What is death? Do we know the map of this next city? Are we ready for it? If we are not ready for it, then we are not ready for this world. Allah *says: 'If you are blind in this world, you will be blind in the next...'* [17:72]. The next world is much more subtle. We cannot act anymore. The Prophet says, '*We die according to how we live and we will be resurrected according to our death.*' So be prepared. It doesn't mean we will be miserable. We will be joyful because we know that the whole thing is passing. So we are in the kindergarten. We know there is one master. Whoever remembers death all the time does not become morose. The remembrance of death is also the door to inner joy in this world. This world will be a stepping stone to the next world. But we have to make the journey ourselves. Nobody can give it to us.

☼   Allah says: 'You cannot guide those whom you love...' [28:56]

Even those in the most powerful positions cannot be guided. They have to do it themselves. How? By resorting to Allah. So the door to the higher is opened by accepting and recognizing the lower, recognizing we are weak and forgetful. Allah wanted this. He is the creator of memories. He is the creator of forgetfulness.

The door of supplication is, first and foremost, humility, helplessness, true and utter reliance on Allah, knowing that everything is in His hand. Our forgetfulness is in His hand. According to *shari'ah* we are accountable. But in *haqiqah*, in truth, He has invented and designed forgetfulness so that it occurs at a certain time and we enter through that door. *Shaytan* was subject to Allah. But technically, outwardly, as an entity he disobeyed Allah. So did Allah not know that this entity was going to disobey? What kind of a Creator is He who doesn't know what is going to happen and what is happening. But because that entity had elevated himself and claimed to be of a higher element than Adam, and so it decided to disobey. Allah knew that he would be disobedient. Allah did not make him disobedient. The good and bad is created and we have to choose the good and avoid the bad. In themselves, these moralities, these ethical values, can only become meaningful when they are attached to a situation.

Generosity is Allah's attribute. We too want to be generous. We naturally seek to be constantly closer and closer to perfection, which is another of Allah's attributes. But every generosity, as far as we are concerned, has got to be taken in its context. We cannot be over-generous to a child by overfeeding him chocolate – that is foolish and the opposite of generosity. An act of courage is courage when we truly sacrifice and we know that there may eventually be a big price to pay – we may even die – but we are doing it in the way of Allah. This is courage. Otherwise, it becomes adventurism, foolhardiness or cowardice.

The attributes to which we all aspire are the balanced attributes of, first and foremost, modesty, which w can define as knowing what is enough for us. In fact this is also the root of wealth. The ultimate wealth is to know that we have had enough. Allah is *Ar-Razzaq*, the Provider. We need modesty, containment and contentment.

Without contentment we cannot knock on the door of joy. Without contentment we cannot open the door of knowledge because we are already covered with our anxieties, seeing through our distorting lens. The Prophet advises us that if we are not humble, that is, if we are not visualizing the immensity of Allah, we should at least pretend to be. In the same vein I would say pretend to be content. We will begin to see things more correctly and then we will begin to act correctly. So, modesty is the foundation.

Then there is courage. The two powers in us are to attract and to repulse. Attraction brings about greed and its antidote is modesty. Repulsion is anger but if we transfer it into courage, then it becomes a force for positive change and not destruction. Courage and modesty are the foundations for the best of characters. From them come wisdom. Without these two characteristics there is no wisdom and without these three traits there is no justice. If there is no modesty, no courage and no wisdom, justice becomes personal justice as we are experiencing it in the world– every minute a 'different' type of justice.

Supplication to Allah requires us to be wholesome in all our qualities. With courageous we know that in giving up our life it is not ours. And then wisdom is when we know that all of so called experience will pass. We find the instant becomes for us like thousands of years and so we will have cracked the secret of time and the prison of space by Allah's *rahmah*, because Allah's *nur* is in our *rūh*. That *rūh* is constantly asking to be liberated and it suffers because the *nafs* is being a rascal – *shaytan*! But once the *nafs* yields to the *rūh*, then it becomes an amenable helpmate. Then it is the right marriage.

These are the foundations of our *dīn*. As human beings, our nature is humble. Allah's nature is glorious. We understand His glory. We need to appeal to that. How? We need to be empty so that we reflect it. When we are sick we call upon *ya Shafi* (O Healer).

Allah says: '*My* rahmah *covers every situation*'. When we begin to see that and taste it, then we are yielding to His program. His program is *sibghat'ullah* (literally the 'dyeing in the colors of Allah'). So if we want to have *shifa*, we have to bring the wave band of healing into us. We have to resonate it by our thoughts and actions. Otherwise it will not work. Once, when there was famine in North Africa, one of Shaykhs was asked to come out and pray to the All-Generous. He told the petitioners to wait for two hours. After two hours he came out and they prayed. Within a few hours rain came. The people asked him: 'What happened during these two hours?' He said: 'I had stuff in my house. I had food. I had provisions. I had to remove it or give it away. Otherwise, how could I ask Allah?' How can we ask the All-Generous, unless we allow the vibrancy of that stream of generosity to overtake us?

As part of our incredible heritage in our *dīn* we have the example of the glorious people that went before us. The example of all these '*awliyā*' are available. But who are the followers? Are there people who want this transformation? Or do we want to still talk about information? And look at Allah's *rahmah* now: global events in the last two or three months have given the Muslims an opportunity to wake up to our true heritage so that we become truly '*abd Allah* and therefore Muhammadi in every sense of the word.

The same applies to the other parts of the world: they are all Allah's children, even though they have not had the advantage which we who are born Muslim have had. Every day, every instant, can teach us. Every instant can be an opportunity. Every disaster can become a great opportunity, depending which way you look at it. These great global disasters can be ways to remind each other that what matters is our inner condition. If we do not wake up to that we will pay a heavy price. By being contained, by being content, we are already in the garden. The garden is in us. The outer world is reflecting in our mirror. If our mirror is not sound, the image reflected back will be all cracked. But if we have an eye for it, if we have inner vision, we will see the order inside chaos.

Allah has created this life so that we will awaken and recognize the source of all.

18: CELEBRATING ISLAM

When a religion is a way of life & wellbeing, then its acts of worship are all celebratory.

As Muslims we know that we have a path, a way of life, that is the most perfect and the most usable under every circumstance, by every human being and at all times. We know that the prophetic unveiling of the *Qur'ānic* gift and the way of life of the Prophet Muhammad is such that if we adopt it and live it, we will have a safe journey in this world and an acceptable, agreeable, delightful arrival in the next.

A *mu'min* believes that we have not been created in this world just out of whimsicality; the *mu'min* believes that this world has a purpose and that our bodies, minds and hearts are instruments through which we realize and live the perfect and expected purpose. If we have faith then *Allah* will lead us and guide us in order to reach a point of knowledge whereby *Islam* is the path of success.

We notice, however, so many disappointments and therefore so many Muslims are pessimistic, unhappy and confused and, in many ways, aggressive and disturbed. The foundation for the present situation in the world is the same as it has always been. It is very simple: Discord and conflict arises with creation because creational manifestation is based on opposites which complement each other – this life, the next life; our inner, our outer; meaning and form. At this moment in time during this talk, we need to listen in order to enhance our inner knowledge. We are concerned about meaning. We want to know how this world, this earth or this cosmos is ruled and governed. Therefore, we need to sit quietly and have least involvement in or concern about our form, which is the body. Everything in this life is based on this dualism of inner-outer, meaning-form, earthly-heavenly. This business of discord or conflict, therefore, is a natural condition of existence. You breathe in, you breathe out. On the face of it, these two breaths are opposites, but in reality they complement each other and they meet.

Our habits of worship are the same thing. There is constriction and expansion. During the month of *Ramadān*, there is constriction, essentially abstention from material input such as food or drink or other things, but equally if not far more important is abstention from mental input or disturbance, so that we restrict the poison that comes to us all the time from the work place, from the *dunya*. The *dunya* is a stepping stone to the *ākhirah*. We need both. We do not deny *dunya*. We deny attachment to it, excessive involvement or obsession with it. This is what we need to deny, so that we are in this *dunya*, but not overwhelmed by it. This is the reason to celebrate that we Muslims have the code; whether we live it or not is another issue.

Over the past two or three hundred years, western civilization gave excessive attention to the outer form through science, technology, materialism and inventions to do with material services, money markets, finance and so on. By about 150 years ago they had taken the whole world and are still exploiting it. Anything they look at, they immediately think how they can utilize it, whether it is a tree or a cow or a human being. How can it be useful for us to earn more and make more? This obsession with possession has now become global. And many of us Muslims have taken on that ethos. We are *Jum'ah* Muslims: we go once a week to the mosque and find ourselves so far from that delight.

Why or how has this happened? Simple life has now been replaced by a very complicated system of governance. A hundred years ago there were hardly any so-called Muslim countries. There were

Muslim communities. There were Muslim towns and cities. Many urban enclaves had someone who, though not the political ruler, was probably the wisest or most enlightened person. Even the rulers would have listened to them. But this is no longer the case. With central governments, we now have despotic rulers, pretending that they are also following in the footsteps of the Prophet Muhammad. That is why we are ashamed in many ways whenever we identify ourselves with some of our, so-called, misleading leaders.

It is not the fault of Islam. It is the fault of our not having committed ourselves to transformation but to a love of information, which has very little connection with transformation and being enlivened by the prophetic way of life. However, I am exceptionally optimistic and I see the brightest future for *Islam*. The reason is simple: the Western pursuit of materialism has almost reached its limit. There is nowhere further to go. There is not a piece of the sky or the earth or the ocean that has not been abused and exploited and over fished and over poisoned by gas. So, after that where do we go?

We are seeing the peak of a new human arrogance: that we are in control. If we look at anything, we need to know how we can use it, abuse it, and exploit it and so on. From this extreme, there can only be the alternative view, asking why we should have more. Indeed, in the West nowadays, we find people becoming minimalists in many fields of business, industry and of course the health sciences – less is being understood as better. The so-called upward mobility that western education has pushed people into over the last few decades really implies outward increase and outward increase has to bring inward decrease because we are all one person.

If we spend 20 hours a day exploiting, exploring or being concerned with the outer, we have no time for our hearts. I am so optimistic for *Islam* because the definition, the theory as well as the practice of 'who are we?', works. You are *rūh* within a body that is a kingdom. If we rule over that kingdom, then we are representing the

One and Only ruler. If we are correct and courteous to our bodies, our senses, our minds, and our intellects, then we are living according to the intended way of a *khalifah*: ready to leave this world and ready to take our responsibility. Serve others who are less fortunate than ourselves and we will begin to discover that there is no otherness. We are all the same: we all want contentment, peace, everlasting joy, happiness. This does not come by the constant pursuit of the outer – wanting more and more, and greater control over everything.

A hundred years ago colonialism was based on brute force. Now it is entirely based on electronic withdrawal of a certain IMF Funding or World Bank funding. It is far more effective colonialism without a face to it – 'You are now no longer desirable. Out you go!' So change of government, change of regime can be indirectly controlled. This imbalance, this constant, continuous, excessive outward emphasis will come to an end because we are all the same human beings. It is not that somebody in Mexico or in America or in Germany is not also seeking the same thing. Everyone is seeking reliable happiness. But when everybody is put through the mill of constant dependence on insurance and reinsurance and outer security, they will end up being inwardly insecure. People cannot have greater outward security than by preferring the western systems, but the majority of them are inwardly insecure. The more they accumulate, the more they become vulnerable because they get so used to that power and mimicking God in that ultimate power that they cannot conceive any reduction, whereas we Muslims celebrate reduction. *Salāt* is nothing other than reduction – acknowledging that Allah is greater than we can ever think or imagine, and therefore we are nothing.

We will fail as Muslims if we do not see the *rahmaniyya* in every situation. If we are businessmen and we have lost a deal and we do not see the *rahmah* in that, it means that for those times, those moments we have left the prophetic path because:

☼   Allah says, '...and My mercy encompasses all things; so I will ordain it (specially) for those who cautiously guard (against evil) ...' [7:156]

These are the transformative elements of our *dīn*. If we truly live by them we will be alive and this life will only be a small reflector of eternal life to which we return after leaving that which is not ours: the so-called body and the incredible dominion within it. How can we not celebrate this submission? How can any intelligent person not be thrilled at what Allah has given them, which is beyond generosity? But if we are looking for pleasures, then we will equally pay a price for displeasure. These are Allah's laws and we are not going to change them simply because we have the name of Muhammad or Ali or whatever. We will be subjected to the same laws out of Allah's constant, perpetual generosity and love for all His creation.

Therefore, we have to tread gently in this world. We are guests of Allah. It is not only when we are going to *hajj* that we recite '*Allahuma labayk*' a few times. We are in His thrall all the time. Did we invent the air and the balance between oxygen and all the other gases in it? Do we know how many miles of blood capillaries we have in us? Are we aware that our hearts beat a hundred thousand times a day? We take it all for granted and move clumsily. We are not sensitive enough to the great kingdom we have been given custody of – our body, the senses, both the gross and the subtle. All of it is permeated by *Al-Latif*, the subtle power of Allah, through the *rūh*.

We are a *rūh* caught in a body, in order for the *rūh* to be realized and recognized. That is why we love the peace of good sleep and the comfort of good companionship. We do not want to be constantly disturbed and given bad news – bad news is discord. Most of us live discordantly, however, between our heart and our mind. The two need to be unified. If the mind follows the program already lodged within each of us to seek the permanent, to seek Allah's perfection it will realize and see Allah's generosity even when we are being constricted. This is cause for celebration. And the *Eid* celebration after the month of *Ramadān* marks in a small way we have achieved abstention, and therefore we have managed to mimic *As-Samad*, the Eternally Self- subsistent. A little abstention gives the body and mind a rest. Even though the fasting makes it hard to remain sharp mentally, and some even become irritable, even so, we experience a surge in self-awareness.

The entire business is to do with awareness of our conduct. We only have one heart. We can only act in one direction. It may not be the right time and place. It may not be the right manner. Our own inner psyche may be disturbed. So we should wait until we are calm and then we do it in the name of Allah – *bismillah*. All of it is *bismillah*, even when we are acting arrogantly. Arrogance is created by Allah in order to humble us and humiliate us to return to the path. There is nothing in existence unless it can be seen in a positive light. Indeed, for the real Muslim man and woman whatever mistake they make can be the key that opens up the door of virtue through their suffering from that mistake, not wanting to do it again and then they will be aware of the pitfall into which they had fallen many times. So it is *rahmah* upon *rahmah*, generosity upon generosity. This is where celebration comes.

If there are enough individuals committed to being enlightened, then there will be an enlightened community. Otherwise we end up talking about community and *ummah* and accuse everybody else without having done our own homework on our own transformation. We end up with a lot of information, a lot of accusations, but insufficient spiritual growth and development.

My optimism extends to the western world. Although it has gone through a period of high-handed, materialistic, abusive, neo-colonization, westerners are also human beings. They are also the sons of Adam. In a sense, they have gone too far, but from that suffering will come the ever-present divine offering. A few years ago they classified human beings according to color – now no longer. Your status now is very much according to the amount of money you have or according to IQ, which has been replaced by EQ. This emotional intelligence has already been replaced by SQ or spiritual intelligence, meaning referring to the highest. Everything else is relative. But we are seeking something that is permanent, which is the divine precinct in your heart. That is the *nur* of Allah. Otherwise, we end up religious, superstitious, and everybody thinks he has the right religion and nobody else has it.

The hope is that Allah's presence, Allah's Light, Allah's ways have always been the paramount, dominant factor and force in this life. It is up to us to embrace it, follow it, submit to it and be in true Islam. We will be thrilled how Allah is forgiving, how Allah is accepting. But we have to pay a price for our mistakes – a tiny price. A good deed will wipe out so many wrong deeds. Allah says, *'Any good deed will be multiplied ten times.'* What generosity! So, when we fail or fall, we should take that as a good sign and resolve within us that we do not want to suffer. No human being wants anything other than everlasting joy.

☼ Allah says: 'Do men think that they will be left alone on saying, We believe, and not be tried?' [29:2]

Allah does not need testing and trying. It is we who need testing as we evolve. I said I like to be generous, but have I really been generous? I like to donate, but donate for what? Who is the giver? All of it is from Allah; at best we can be conduits, small flashes representing the *rahmah* of Allah. These are the qualities that a *mu'min* will absorb from the *Qur'ān*. Then the community will also absorb these qualities.

☼   '...Who fears the Beneficent Allah in the Unseen and comes with a heart returning (in penitence)...' [50:33]

The qualifications must be right. It is no use wanting to drive well without using the map, simply relying on the fact that *'alhamdu li'llah* we are Muslim'. We have to be accountable, responsible and responsibility begins with ourselves, not putting on a 'face'.

People in the West have not had the prophetic teaching in a clear way. They went through the renaissance and the reformation, much confusion and warfare. It therefore ended up quite rationally, quite expectedly secular. But we do not need to do that. We Muslims have to behave ourselves and return to the early days of *Rasūl Allah*. Imagine yourself in Makkah, surrounded by enemies, ignorant and arrogant Arabs. Imagine yourself in that situation and you will find that others are really the same as you – your brothers and sisters. The more we are instantly aware of our intention, we become ready for departure. Whoever is ready for departure is qualified for arrival. If not, we are out of balance. So we celebrate our *dīn*; we celebrate the prophetic path. We celebrate the clarity that we have been given by the glorious Prophet who summed up what went on before him, and equally we have such a rich heritage from the great people who came after the *Tābi'ūn*, and later on the *Awliyā'*, the *imams,* the *Ahl ul-Bayt* and the great enlightened *Shuyukh* of the various *tariqahs*.

The world now has reached a point of globalization and so will *Islam*. The Prophet said, *'Islam began as a stranger to the people to whom it came...'* Initially people resisted claiming Islam was too different from what their forefathers practiced. The message the Prophet gave was that these ways have to be renewed. We must accept the culture that we have come from – Indian, Pakistani, Turkish – and the schools of law (*madhhab*), for it does not matter. Accept it and move beyond it. Get back to the companionship of *Rasūl Allah*. Without accusation or recrimination. We may feel better for a moment but we will feel miserable for the rest of our lives.

Forgive your parents. Forgive those who went before us. Forgive the ignorance of the Muslim leadership and move on. Otherwise, we remain oppressed under a burden of historical consciousness that has been accumulated and which is impossible for us to work out. Forgive them, as Allah is All-Forgiving. We should care for our real self, which is your heart. We should not put anything in our heart. Allah talks of: *'he between whom and you was enmity would be as if he were a warm friend'* [41:34]. If we don't do that it means that our heart is full of poison and pus. We have to have love for others who have less than us, who are less competent, less able.

We should be understanding and compassionate, for Allah is the Compassionate. We have to imitate Allah. If we love the divine names, then we love all those attributes which we need to take a little of – generosity, patience and compassion. This is the path to celebrate, enjoy and be joyful about and at the same time be concerned and cautious. We should not arrogantly boast that *alhamdu li'llah*, we did a lot of *tarawih* and so on. Allah does not need that. Allah wants you to abandon totally unto Him as you were in the womb and as you will one day be in the tomb. This is a cause of delight, not heaviness. We have responsibility for ourselves first and every other self is the same. Allah's decree is pairs and pairs and pairs but one self. He also says: *'Within that self lays the* Shaytan, *but the light of* Rahman *ever shining is also there.'* Turn to the *Rahman* and avoid the *Shaytan*. We have made use of *Shaytan*, but it has also made use of us.

We have the map; if we don't want to drive along it nothing will happen. By driving cautiously – *bismillah, bismillah* – we will find that Allah's *Rahmah* was always there, but we were looking somewhere else.

'There is no situation that does not encompass the Mercy of Allah'

19: THE WAY FORWARD

All human beings wish to have a quality of life now as well as in the future.

☼   'Have we not expanded your breast for you? And alleviated your burden for you, which had so heavily weighed down your back? And raised up for you your remembrance? For certainly with every difficulty there is ease, certainly, with every difficulty there is ease. So when you are freed (of occupations), remain steadfast, expend! And make your Lord your exclusive object [of Longing]. [94:1-8]

Allah addresses the Prophet Muhammad, and therefore all the Muslims who follow the Prophetic way, to think back and consider all the problems he had had in the past that were no longer there. Consider your own situation: concerns you once had are no longer the same. Has your breast not been expanded? Do you not feel that the burdens you considered in the past are no longer there?

The entire business of creation and of journeying in this life is to feel light-hearted, not to feel obsessed, depressed and overwhelmed or any other negative feelings and tendencies that we experience. Allah reminds us through the perfect model and the paradigm of the prophetic being-*ness*, so He says: *'Don't you see you are relieved now?'* And then all that we consider to be burdens and difficulties are over. If we are following the path of enlightenment through faith and appropriate action, no doubt every one of us will realize frequently how the burdens disappear.

The questions do not always get answered in the way you expect it. More often they simply dissolve. Their validity ceases. For example, if you were planning a house with four or five storeys and you suddenly were struck with a form of paralysis, you would not be able to do live in that home. Something else takes over. Different priorities change your attitude and your mindset. It is as if Allah is saying consider this whole world is to do with constant evolving, changing, and striving towards the knowledge of Him whose light is in you which is called the *rūh*. We are all seeking Allah. Allah says: *'I created jinn and mankind only to worship Me'* [51:56]

Worship implies adoration. Adoration implies love. Love implies that you already know the object of your wish and desire for proximity thereof. You desire wealth, Allah is the source of all wealth – *huwa'l-Ghani*. You desire power – *huwa'l-Qawi*. You desire subtle sensitivities and understanding – *huwa'l-Latif.* You desire longevity – *huwa'l-Bāqi*. All the attributes that we yearn for are divine attributes. That is the meaning of, *'And Allah's are the most beautiful names, so invoke Him by them ...'* [7:180]

These are the names, attributes and qualities that every human being loves. You are in the *mihrāb* of worshipping Allah's perfect qualities, you therefore like any human being who is more forgiving because Allah is all-Forgiving – *al-Ghafūr*. Since Allah is the all-Generous – *Al-Karim*, human beings warm to someone who is generous. If the self (*nafs*) takes on a little of the qualities of the higher, this means it is yielding to and obeying the higher. Indeed, all obedience means is to obey the perfect qualities that we praise. That is why we say *al-hamdu li'llah* – which literally means: the praise belongs to Allah, and by extension we are praising Allah's attributes. We can have a little of some of His attributes such as clemency (*huwa'l-Halim*). Or if we want to hear well then it is the all-Hearing (*huwa's-Sami*) we attune to. There are some qualities we cannot have anything of, e.g. the Almighty, the Glorious (*huwa'l-Aziz*). How can the *nafs*, 'I' who have only been born in order to die, have this glory? So the *nafs* must take the opposite quality: humility. You and I must practice humility, not pride.

The Muslim world's suffering now is due to misplaced pride. Monsters have been created in the Middle East. The nation of Iraq, to which I belong, has the glory of Islam still strong alive in our minds. Our history was in parts glorious, but equally very patchy and darks on other parts. But we human beings have this selective memory: we choose all the nice parts and identify with them, whilst our own life is not up to that standard. Therefore we want somebody else to give us pride and we invent such monsters as our despots of whom we have many, the last one being the last deposed ruler of Iraq. He had pride. Pride based on what? All of our goods and products have emanated from the West. We despise the *kufr* (hypocritical, double standard) system, but yet we are living with and loving all their products. If we put these two together, we end up with a schizophrenic personality, completely unable to match the two parts. If we do not realize the illness and the state we are in, how can we go forward with success?

The way forward is based on understanding our present challenges, difficulties, dilemmas and dealing with them correctly, with reason, counsel, patience, persistence and with perseverance. The future then is always going to be better. All human beings are endowed with the desire to be hopeful. Otherwise you would not get out of bed in the morning! When I first came on my early visits to Africa in the early nineties, the African people had no hope. The majority of the people in this land, native Africans, were hopeless and despondent. Look at them now. Most faces I see now are hopeful. They are smiling. There is some improvement. There are opportunities. They can be educated. They can compete.

Without hope we will not be able to express any of the positive tendencies we want to have – expecting the best, that tomorrow will be better. There is no such thing as being a 'failure'. The project has failed. You are not the project. You are Allah's project to know His attributes, His perfections and constantly do your best to see His perfections. See the perfection of your failure in the interview – you had certain expectations, you had already rehearsed it in your mind, and suddenly the interviewer did not care for all of that. You went in with a neck tie, a nice briefcase and all that and it turns out he is a hip employer and not impressed by traditional office suits. He judges you to be insufficiently creative and you don't get the job. Once you realize the inappropriateness of that event, you will see the failure is not attached to you. Failure implies that the right thing, the expected thing, did not happen at that moment, meaning it was not appropriate.

Our love for the Prophet Muhammad (S) is because he always acted appropriately. Appropriateness means that at that instant there was perfection, whether he said something or he was silent or whichever way he behaved. It meant that at that moment, there was balance, equilibrium, goodness and there was tranquility, all of which again are divine attributes. We are caught by the ever-perfection of Allah's qualities. And yet, you and I can never attain perfection for more than a minute. As soon as you get your health together, your mind is somewhere else! There is always outer change in the world. We have planned and prepared that our family will grow well. Suddenly, we find drugs are being sold in the neighborhood. So we bring back into focus the principle of living this life in preparation for the next without denying this life, living it accountably at all times, constantly aware of our responsibility, seeing other people as our brothers and sisters, if not better than us. These are the qualities of the followers of Prophet Muhammad.

The times have changed in the world. So what are we going to do? Are we going to change the *Qur'ān*? Are we going to change the perfection of the Prophet's way? We cannot do that. Primal values will never change. The goodness of the mother's unconditional love will never change. The goodness of a man of honor who is at all times ready to give up everything to Allah and be silent before death will never change. The goodness of generosity will never change. The goodness of helping other human beings, no matter who they are, will never change. Only the way you and I are going to act will change, not the values.

The goodness in that you are available when I am sick, to greet me or to help me or to give me energy will never change. You may come on a donkey or maybe you will come by car – this may change. The way you communicate with me, if it was by letter then, now it may be by e-mail. The means have changed, but the content that we desire is always the same.

The way forward is about moving towards a situation in which you and I will never ever be disappointed. That means dealing with this world with reasoning, counsel, wisdom and with knowledge, but also constantly being aware of the hereafter (*ākhirah*) – the two go together. Your life in the future is based on living your world as best as you can, landscaping and planting up a garden for the Hereafter (*mazra'ah li'l-ākhirah*) – as the Prophet described, a little orchard in which you plant the seeds by experience, by *'amal, 'amal, 'amal,* (action, action, action), so that when you leave this world, this prison, then you are free. In this world, the only freedom accessible is in your heart. Outwardly, we are subject and accountable to *shar'iāh*, to limits and boundaries – no freedom. Allah says:

> ☼ 'Surely man is created of a hasty temperament, Being greatly grieved when evil afflicts him, And niggardly when good befalls him, Except those who pray, Those who are constant in their prayer, And those in whose wealth there is a fixed portion, for him who begs and for him who is denied (good).' [70: 19-25]

If you have wealth or power it means you have responsibility. You are a custodian. What is this business of favoritism and nepotism with our leaders and sultans? That methodology has spawned a mess. It does not work. You must be accountable to the Truth (*haqq*). Where is justice? Where is *'adl*? *'Adl* is the middle path: correct balance. *'Adalah*, or justice, will only come to human beings after *hikmah*, wisdom. Wisdom cannot occur unless you are modest and also courageous. These are the qualities that will always work for you, whatever you are doing, wherever you are, whoever you are.

The way forward, therefore, is based on your being equipped for the changes that will take place. Equipped with what? Essentially: faith and trust in Allah, that Allah has created this world and all the forces according to perfection. If you see its perfection within them, then you will not feel all the misery and the sorrow that most other people do. Returning to and living our *Qur'ān* is what we need. Listen to the following *Qur'ānic* verses:

☼   'Do the people think that they will be left to say,
We believe, and they will not be tried?' [29:2]

In other words, if you claim to be a *mu'min* or a *muslim*, are you assuming you will not be afflicted and tested? Allah is not there to afflict you for fun. Being tested is for our own sake, to see how we have deviated. If I am devoted to a project or a business and it does not work and my reaction is sorrow or anger, this is affliction. If I stop and see the meaning behind it – 'what is Allah's message?' – it may well be that had that business started, in few years time it would have been worse off than others, deeper in debt and more stressed. So how do you know that the loss now is not more palatable than a later, larger loss? This is to do with faith (*īmān*): I have faith that Allah will guide me as to what is appropriate for me.

Then we are reminded: '*Certainly with every difficulty comes ease...*' [94:5-6]. Often outer difficulties for the believer (*mu'min*) are doorways to inner ease. You find you have time on your hands. Reflect back. What can you do to free yourself from being captured entirely by your images and mindset? And then Allah gives us the ultimate secret: wherever you are, whoever you are, you will win by Allah as the winner because *hūwa'l-Ghālib*. 'And there is no other winner except Allah' (*wa lā ghāliba illa'llah*). If you submit your project to Allah's ways, you will always see His help (*nasr*). You will always taste victory.

> ☼ 'O you who believe! answer (the call of) Allah and His Messenger when he calls you to that which gives you life; and know that Allah intervenes between a man and his heart, and that to Him you shall be gathered.' [8:24]

Meaning: 'Those of you who have faith and trust that you will come to know the purpose of this life, follow Allah's ways. Obey Allah, accept His ways and His patterns and avoid what He has asked you to avoid; and then follow the Prophet, answer him when he calls you to that which is going to give you life.'

The key to the ayah is, 'when he calls you to that which gives you life' (*idhā da'ākum li-mā yuhyikum*). Da'wah is calling people to the *dīn*, but ultimately it is Allah who is calling us to His light, which He has also given us a glimpse of, or a flash of, as a *rūh*. Essentially we are made of light and matter. Matter is only an indicator of the light. Respect the body and matter because it has come about because of Allah's Light (*nur*), which is the *rūh* in us. Human life, therefore, is sacred, because it is activated, energized and alive by Allah's command of 'Be' (*Kun*). Therefore, if the heart is clear we have access to our *rūh*. And the *nafs* indicates it. As I said earlier, we love generosity because the *rūh* has in it the patterns of the all-Generous. We despise meanness because it is the shadow side, or the other side, of generosity. This is the cosmology of the self (*nafs*). Allah says:

☼   'And the soul and Him Who made it perfect, Then He inspired it to understand what is right and wrong for it' [91: 7-9]

Taqwa (cautious awareness at several levels of human consciousness) is to like generosity, obedience, to do our *salāt* on time, follow the rules, stop, and abstain. And the opposite of it, it is *fujūr* (meanness, decadence, corruption, breakdown and lack of awareness).

The *rūh* on the other hand is from the command of Allah (*min amri rabbi*). So if we truly want to be on the path, then we should follow *amri rabbi* and the *rabbi* can only be followed if our hearts allow us to constantly bask in the light of the *rūh*. Therefore the heart must be pure and clear. If the heart is full of pus, the love of this world (*dunya*), then we are as good as that. But if we are consciously connected to the *nur* that has created the *dunya*, then it is the *dunya* plus. Do not deny the *dunya*. Deny your attachment to it. Deny being under it. There is nothing wrong with the *dunya* if it leads us to the Hereafter (*ākhirah*). But once it has become the all-consuming obsession, then we are blocked. Then we have no light. Then we become constantly gloomy according to the money we have or don't have.

The next verse gives us the entire secret of the way forward:

☼   'Whoever does good whether male or female and he is a believer, We will most certainly make him live a happy life, and We will most certainly give them their reward for the best of what they did.' [16:97]

Doing righteousness or good work means acting without expectation, doing it for your highest sake, for Allah's sake. When we say *fi sabili'llah*, Allah does not need us. It is we who have assumed now we are on the *sabil* of Allah. Be careful that it does not become arrogant boast – that 'I have built this mosque, I have given.' That again becomes another false and more dangerous arrogance – 'I know more than you, I read the *Qur'an* more than you.' It is not about *more*. It is about submission to the truth and not seeing the *nafs* and only being guided by the *rūh*. This is a subtle matter. It is to do with Islamic courtesy to be modest. Do not see yourself; and if you see your *rūh*, you will see everybody else has a *rūh* and so we accept them as human beings. We should not elevate ourselves. Whoever does good work, the work that leads to knowledge, the work that leads us to be the servant of Allah (*'abd Allah*), that leads us to be fully present in the moment (*'abdu'l-waqt*), that leads us to strive constantly to do the right thing at the right time, in the right way, with no past and no future, will taste a joyful life.

Whether male or female, if they have faith and trust (*īmān*), whoever does this will come to live, meaning they will realize life is forever – (*fal-nuhiyannahū hayātan tayyibatan*). Our love of foreverness is a small reflection of the *rūh* which continues forever. Because we know that though the body is not forever, the *rūh* is forever, we are relieved from fear of death. The Prophet reminds us all the time to remember death because it will reduce our hankering for pleasures as it is the destroyer of pleasure. Every pleasure will give us displeasure until we are illumined. Once at the door of bliss it is no longer a matter of pleasure or displeasure; it is joy – the joy of knowing that essentially we are a *rūh* caught for a while in space and time in order to realize that and realize its *Rabb*, its creator – Lord of all the worlds (*rabbi'l-'ālamin*). Then we witness perfection at all times.

Allah reminds us in the *Qur'an* to travel in the land and see what has happened to those so-called great civilizations. Whenever things grow it is because of *tawhīd* – seeing the One, acting by the One, being responsible to the One, then putting up with and accepting the manifestations of the twos. Without that, nobody could accept anyone else. Once we have seen the light of the One, then we will find others are our brothers and sisters, at different levels of unveilings and arrival and knowledge. Enlightenment is the only thing we can truly desire and we will never go wrong with that desire, for enlightenment means seeing the One light from which emanate multiple manifestations and infinite varieties. Go for the One, the two will be alright and the multiples will be alright. Try and make sense out of the many and you will lose everything. The way forward for an individual and a society is none other than enlightenment in the magnificence of the now.

If we believe Allah's action and Allah's patterns are perfect, then there is even perfection in the misery we experience now. Use the occasion in which the Muslims are under attack globally to rise to the honor of living Islam. Otherwise we will constantly denounce each other and feel nostalgic and throw accusations around. They are accountable to their Creator, just as we are accountable now to the ever-present Creator and to each other.

The question begging an answer is what are we doing to be worthy of being illumined Muslims – that is, to be enlightened, in the presence of Allah, the Lord of majesty and honor (*dhū'l jalāli wa'l-ikrām*), humble, but honored as a being created as a child of Adam? We could have been any other animal. Allah could have created us in all kinds of other forms. Here we are, with reasonable bodies and reasonable minds; we can access our *rūh* through clear hearts. Give that which you want to keep and are attached to so that you are free from it and then you will see wonder upon wonder. Then you will find the subtle and the gross meet.

When we see a door that is closed, we see the *rahmah* of Allah in its closure. We don't become angry and accuse everybody else. Then we are truly the servant of Allah (*'abd Allah*). If there is more available for us in this world, the greater is our responsibility. If there is less, we are free. Then it is not about the wealth we have: it is about the extent of our attachment and love of it. That is all it is. Are we practicing freedom from the body, ready for the time or the moment that comes for us to leave this world or are we acting more and more as though we are the wealthy (*al-Ghani*)?

There is nothing wrong with things in themselves. What is wrong is the relationship we have with them. It is the same thing with virtue. A virtue is a virtue by virtue of it being perfect at that moment. What if someone gives sugar to a sick person who is going to die of diabetes? Sugar and sweets often symbolize treats, but where is the generosity in that act? So it is appropriateness that defines the virtuousness of any act – at that moment, withholding sugar is generosity. We have to be as our Prophet was, acting appropriately. When we look back on history people can criticize. They knew how to act but could not do it. At that moment it could be that there was no other course of action better than that. Therefore, the circumstances of traditions are important. Utterances taken out of context lose half if not all their meaning.

The important thing affecting the history (*sirah*) of the Prophet was the environmental factors. What else could he do when he was surrounded by enemies not accepting him as messenger of Allah (*Rasūl Allah*)? During the writing of Sulh al-Hudaibiyyah, the peace pact with Makkah, he instructed the scribes to erase '*Rasūl Allah*' from the letter, but once they had a community, they declared they were honored to have *Rasūl Allah* amongst them and reinstated it. It is not a matter of abrogation or saying this is right and this is wrong; it is appropriateness.

During the early years in Makkah, our glorious Prophet was surrounded by enemies, most of whom were his own family. So his work was mostly reminding people about death, about accountability, about illumination. Later on when there was a community, they had to preserve the dignity of family, people, women and so on, who were given honor by our predecessors. But later on we sank into assuming we are good Muslims whilst still practicing some sort of a culturalized, highly structured religion, completely unaware of the innate nature of the never-changing light of the *Qur'ān* and the way of the Prophet.

The way forward is to aim for a situation where we are beyond hope, beyond good and bad, beyond any of these matters because we are with Him who has created the duality of the world as a way to return to divine Unity (*tawhīd*) and the oneness that permeates all of these worlds.

Without *tawhīd* there is no future for anyone. The present western civilizations will collapse or deteriorate according to whether they are going to rediscover and give into the one Creator Who is challenging them and live this world in preparation for the next, or to continue their own fancy ways of aggrandizement, building taller and bigger buildings – which our own people in the so-called Muslim world are mimicking with much less efficiency. We must see things as they are.

It is no use blaming this or that or this school of opinion (*madhhab*). We must return to the original *madhhab* of the Prophet, the ultimate glory of the *Qur'ān*, accountability and following those amongst us who know better than us in any fashion. If we want to establish a business, we go to a successful businessman and take his counsel. If we want light, go to the people who have light. If we want a building, go to the best contractor who has already proven he is a good builder and so on. Expect the best and you will get the best. If we are ready to be the servant of Allah (*'abd Allah*) we will be honored by the One and only Giver of everything that we receive.

Mankind's origin is from the Adamic blueprint and thus of One Essence.

GLOSSARY

'Abd Allah (pl. *'ibād Allah*) – servant of Allah

'Abdu'l-waqt – servant of the moment

Adab – courtesy

'Adhāb – punishment

Ādhān – call to prayer

'Adl/'adālah – justice/fairness

'Afuw – pardon

Ahl ul-Bayt – members of the Prophet's (SAW) family

Ahl ul-dunya – people attached to this material world

Ahl ul-jannah – people of the Garden

Ahl ul-kitab – people of the Book

Ākhirah – the hereafter or eternal life

al-'Alīm – the All Knowing – One whose knowledge is infinite

al-Ākhir – the Last

al-Awwal – the First

al-'Azīz – the All Mighty

al-Bāqī – the Everlasting

al-Basīr – the All-seeing

al-Ghālib – the Victorious

al-Ghanī – the Rich beyond need

al-Hakīm – the Most Wise

al-hamdu li'Llāh – expression meaning 'All praise be to Allah'

al-Haqq – the Absolute Truth

'Ālim – a scholar

al-Jalāl – the Majestic

al-Jamāl – the Most Beautiful

al-Karīm – the Most Generous
Allah – Islamic term for God
al-Latīf – the Subtle
al-Mālik – the Master/Owner
al-Murīd – the Willer
al-Qadir – the Most Able
al-Qawī – the most Strong
al-Wahhāb – the Bestower
'Amal as-salih – good/virtuous actions
'Amal – action
ammaratun bi's-su' – see *nafs al-ammarah*
'Aql – intellect
Ard – earth
ar-Rahmān – the All Merciful
ar-Razzāq – the Ever Providing
'Arsh – throne
A.S. – *alayhi's-salam*, 'upon him be peace', usually invoked after the mention of a prophet's name.
as-Sabūr – the Patient
as-Samad – the Eternally Self-Subsistent
as-Samī' – the All-hearing
ash-Shafī' – the Healer
Astaghfiru'llah – asking Allah for the cover of forgiveness
Awliyā' – saints, see *wali*
Āyah – a sign, more specifically a verse or sentence from the *Qur'ān*; pl. *āyāt*.
'Ayn al-yaqīn – eye of certainty
'Azm – steadfastness
Bay'ah – pledge/obedience
Bala' – test/affliction
Barzakh – bridge/intermediate place or interspace (between this life and the next)

Bismi'llah, or Bismillah – In the name of Allah

Da'wah – the call to Islam

Dahr – time

Dīn – way of transacting life

Dhalīl – humble, lowly

Dhikr – remembrance, invocation

Dhikru'llah – remembrance of Allah

Dhu'l-jalali wa'l-ikrām – the Master of Majesty and Nobility

Dhulm – injustice/oppression

Du'a – supplicatory prayer

Dunyā – the temporal world and its concerns and possessions

Fanā' fi'llah – Annihilation of the ego-self in Allah

Fi sabili'llah – In the way of Allah

Fitnah – test/trial, affliction

Fitrah – primordial state/innate nature

Fu'ād – heart, specifically the inner core that never lies.

Ghaflah – distraction, heedlessness

Hadīth – recorded saying or tradition of the Prophet

Hāfiz al-Qur'ān (pl. *Huffaz*) – one who has committed, & thereby protected, the entire *Qur'ān* to memory

Hajj – pilgrimage to Makkah

Hakīm – healer

Halāl – lawful, permitted

Haqiqah – Reality, inner truth

Haqq – truth, reality; *al-Haqq* divine Name

'Haqq al-yaqīn – truth of certainty

Harām – forbidden, harmful

Hayāt – Life

Hijrah – Emigration

Hikmah – wisdom

Hilm – forbearance

Hudūr – presence

Huwa – He is/to whom belongs

I'tikaf – period of seclusion, usually in the *masjid*, for the purpose of worship usually performed during the last 10 days of Ramadan

'Ibādah – worship

Ihsān – Excellent or perfect conduct

Ijtihad – Juridical reasoning, exerting utmost effort in deriving sound legal rulings

Ikhlās – sincerity

'Ilm – knowledge

'Ilm al-yaqīn – knowledge of certainty. Intellectual understanding and appreciation of an event. The first level of awareness of an event.

Imām – leader; therefore prayer leader

Īmān – faith based on trust

Insān – a person or human

Irādah – will

'Irfān – gnosis or inner knowledge

'Ishq – love or yearning for the Divine

Islāh – restoration or correction

Islām – submission; the Arabic root word invokes yielding to reality, obedience, purity and peace

Istighfār – asking for the cover of forgiveness – see *astaghfirullah*

Jahd – negation, denying, refusing

Jannah – paradise, heaven

Jihād – expending/exerting energy

Jizyah – A special tax due to the Muslim treasury from Christians and Jews

Jum'ah – Friday, the day of gathering, hence the Friday congregational prayer

Kāfir – from the word *kafara* – to hide; he who deliberately hides or denies the truth; pl. *kuffār*, unbelievers, deniers or truth

Khalifah – Vice-gerent or steward; he who stands in the place of

Khalwa – seclusion/spiritual retreat

Khayr – Better

Kitāb – book/ *Qur'ān*

Kufr – ungratefulness and disbelief in God and denial of the truth

Kun – God's command 'Be!'

La ilāha illa'llah – There is no god but Allah

Ma'rifah – gnosis, enlightenment

Madhhab – school of jurisprudence; pl. *madhāhib*

Madinah – the City – the town of Yathrib renamed after the Prophet and his followers emigrated there; first Muslim city

Madrasah – school, university

Makkah – the ancient town of Bakkah, home of the Ka'bah

Masjid – place of prayer, mosque

Mazra'ah – Garden, plantation

Mihrāb – prayer niche

Min amri Rabbi – By the command of my Lord

Miskīn – destitute, poor, beggar

Mu'āmalāt – transactions

Mu'min – believer

Muhabbah – love

Muhsin – one who acts and behaves in the best and most appropriate way

Muttaqi – one who is cautiously aware of himself and his actions

Nabīy – prophet, pl. *anbiyā'*

Nafs – the self, the ego

Nafs al-ammārah – the commanding self; *ammaratun bi's-su'* calling to evil

Nafs al-lawwāmah – the reproachful self

Nafs al-mulhamah – the inspired self

Nafs al-mutma'innah – the certain self

Nafs al-rādiyah – the contented self

Nasr – Aid, succor

Nūr – light

Qalb – heart

Qalbun sakin – tranquil heart

Qalbun salīm – contented, wholesome heart

Qarīn – the recording companion

Qiblah – direction of prayer, orientation

Qudrah – power/ability

Qur'ān – book revealed by Allah to the Prophet

Rabb – Lord, Sustainer

Rahmatan li'l-'ālamīn – Mercy to the worlds; epithet of the Prophet (S)

Ramadān – The ninth month of the Islamic calendar, in which fasting is obligatory for all Muslims

Raqīb – the monitoring self

Rasūl – messenger

Rasūl Allah – the Messenger of Allah, i.e. the Prophet Muhammad (S)

Rūh – the soul or spirit

Rūhun wa rayhān – mercy and sweet solace

Sa'ādah – happiness

Sabr – patience

Sahabas – companions of the Prophet

Sajdah – prostration

Salāt – the daily five obligatory prayers

Sālik – seeker

Sawm – fasting

Shāhid – witnesser

Sharī'ah – revealed Code of conduct and law

Shaytān – satan

Shirk – ascribing partners to God

Sibghat Allah – The 'color' of Allah

Sīrah – life or biography of the Prophet (S)

Subhan Allah – 'Glory be to Allah'

Sultan – king/ruler

Sunnah – prophetic practice

Tafsīr – commentary on the *Qur'ān*

Taqwa – cautious or fearful awareness (of Allah) at several levels of human consciousness

Tarīqah – a religious order

Tasbīh – Glorification; name given to an Islamic rosary as a tool for counting glorifications

Tawhīd – Unity, the foundation of all manifested existence, seen or unseen

Tawakkul – total reliance

Tawbah – return/repentance

'Ulamā' – religious scholars

Ummah – nation/community

Walī – saint, also governor in modern Arabic

Wudu' – ablution

Zakāt – obligatory wealth tax

CPSIA information can be obtained
at www.ICGtesting.com
Printed in the USA
LVHW050835140323
741564LV00006B/85